GEOGRAPHY OF RAGE

Printed in Maryland, USA

First Printing: April 2002

Geography of Rage: Remembering the Los Angeles Riots of 1992
Edited by Jervey Tervalon
ISBN 1-893329-23-2
Library of Congress Control Number: 2002091085
10 9 8 7 6 5 4 3 2 1

"April 29, 1992" lyrics by Brad Nowell
©1996 MCA Records Inc.

Cover photograph by Gary Leonard
Cover design by Ingrid Olson, Tülbox Creative Group

Visit our web site at www.ReallyGreatBooks.com

To order *Geography of Rage* or for information on using it for educational purposes, e-mail us at Sales@ReallyGreatBooks.com, or write to:

Really Great Books
P.O. Box 861302
Los Angeles, CA 90086

Really Great Books wishes to thank the following for their permission to reprint versions of materials included in this book.

Shonda Buchanan: "Midnight Cry" originally appeared in the *LA Weekly*. ©1993 by Shonda Buchanan. Reprinted by permission of the author.

Lynell George: "Waiting for the Rainbow Sign" originally appeared in the *LA Weekly*. ©1992 by Lynell George. Reprinted by permission of the author.

Gary D. Phillips: Version of "Destructive Engagment" originally appeared in *CrossRoads magazine*. ©1992 by Gary D. Phillips. Reprinted by permission of the author.

David L. Ulin: "Talkin' Bout A Revolution" originally appeared in the *Pennsylvania Gazette*. ©1992 by David L. Ulin. Reprinted by permission of the author.

GEOGRAPHY OF RAGE
REMEMBERING THE LOS ANGELES RIOTS OF 1992

Jervey Tervalon, Editor
Cristián A. Sierra, Associate Editor

About a year ago I received a call from a producer of "Night Waves", a BBC Radio Show/web program, wanting me to write about the Los Angeles Riot/Uprising. He had been watching the clock; ten years had passed and it was time for us natives to reminisce. I almost felt insulted. A Brit had to offer me money to remember one of the biggest events in the history of one of the most important cities in the world. Why weren't we Los Angelenos talking about it amongst ourselves? Were we that unnerved, shell-shocked that we buried the memories? When I mentioned this to Nina Wiener, a friend and then an editor at Really Great Books, she said that's a book that needs to be written.

To remember: I asked all my friends, writers and nonwriters to recollect how they faced those days of the riots. Without filtering or correctness, but what they saw, or felt; what they ran from, or to. How they slept or partied on.

Something frightening happened ten years ago and it's as though it faded from our memory. We lived through it, were scared and furious, considered bailing on Los Angeles, and feared that this explosion of rage was just the precursor of more unrest. We struggled with the realization that we were being written off by the rest of the country; that Los Angeles was a flawed city from the get go. Had we finally collectively lost it, had a whole city gone tribal on each other? We struggled with the fragmented opinions of how's and why's; the city was too colored, too poor, too vicious, too divided to pull itself back from the abyss of the largest civil disturbance in the history of the United States.

But LA resurrected itself. We got along well enough for the economy to blossom once again, and those that fled to greener or whiter climes were replaced with browner or blacker or yellower faces, and the city didn't miss a beat. It was still too large, too dangerous, too expensive, too smoggy, but we weren't going anywhere.

This is home; a home that almost went up in flames. We need to recollect that ten years later, even if there will be no ten-part documentary on PBS, or Tom Hanks-billed blockbuster recreating with searing realism the fires of '92. We can't watch the revolution in the comfort of our home theaters; better to search our memories for those jagged shards of experience and remember.

—Jervey Tervalon, April 2002

VI

CHRONOLOGY OF RAGE

Cristián A. Sierra

1991

March 3

Rodney Glen King and his passenger, Bryant Allan, are stopped after a freeway pursuit.

Sergeant Stacey C. Koon, Officer Laurence M. Powell, Officer Theodore Briseno, and Officer Timothy Wind begin to deliver fifty-six baton blows and six kicks to King over a two minute period in the presence of seventeen other Los Angeles Police Department (LAPD) officers and four California Highway Patrol (CHP) officers.

George Holliday is awakened by sirens and helicopters. Holliday gets his video camera and walks out onto his balcony and videotapes the beating of King across the street for a total of eighty-one seconds of tape.

Beating ends. King suffers eleven skull fractures and brain and kidney damage.

Police officers file a report stating that King did not stop when signaled but increased his speed to more than 100 miles per hour over the course of 7.8 miles. The report neglected to state that King had sustained any head wounds.

March 4

George Holliday delivers his videotape to Los Angeles television station KTLA.

The videotape is broadcast. By afternoon, international attention is focused on police brutality in the city of Los Angeles.

March 7th

The Los Angeles County District Attorney dismisses all charges against King.

March 15

The four officers involved in the beating of King are charged with assault with a deadly weapon and use of excessive force. The officers are left free on bail pending trial.

March 26

The four officers plead not guilty.

April 1

Mayor Tom Bradley appoints Warren Christopher head of the Independent Commission on the Los Angeles Police Department, also known as the Christopher Commission, to investigate the LAPD.

April 4

Police Chief Daryl Gates, who has civil service protection against being fired, is placed on a sixty day leave by the Christopher Commission.

April 5

The Los Angeles City Council reinstates Gates.

May 7

Gates suspends Sergeant Koon, Officers Powell, and Briseno without pay and fires probationary Officer Wind.

May 10

Seventeen of the officers who stood by as King is beaten escape indictment by a grand jury.

July 9

The Christopher Commission Report calls for the resignation of

Gates and the reform of the LAPD's systematic use of excessive force and racial harassment.

July 22

Gates announces he will retire in 1992.

November 26

Superior Court Judge Stanley Weisberg orders the trial of Koon, Powell, Briseno, and Wind relocated to the conservative and predominantly Anglo community of Simi Valley. The prosecution objects that Simi Valley has different demographics than Los Angeles. Jury selection begins in a neighborhood where many have friends or family who are police officers. The court does not view the probability that many may be biased toward police officers as grounds to dismiss prospective jurors.

1992

March 5

Testimony begins.

April 16

Willie Williams, an African-American and former police commissioner of Philadelphia, is named the successor of Daryl Gates as chief of the LAPD.

April 29

Sergeant Stacey C. Koon, Officer Laurence M. Powell, Officer Theodore Briseno, and Officer Timothy Wind are found not guilty by an all-white jury on all counts except one: Officer Powell, who struck the most blows, is found guilty of excessive force.

Judge Weisberg declares a mistrial on the one count of excessive force.

Riots begin.

Gates leaves LAPD headquarters for a political fundraising party in the affluent beachside community of Pacific Palisades.

Police abandon the intersection of Florence and Normandie in South Central Los Angeles because of heavy rioting.

Choi Sai-Choi, a Chinese immigrant, slows his car because of pedestrian traffic at Florence and Normandie. People rush toward his car, pull him out, beat, and rob him. Choi sustains injuries to his head and lower back. Donald R. Jones, an African-American off-duty firefighter, helps Choi back into his car as looters take Choi's belongings.

Reginald Denny, a white man, is pulled from his truck as he stops to avoid hitting looters. He is beaten at the intersection of Florence and Normandie. He is later given brain surgery to remove a blood clot.

Fidel Lopez, a Guatemalan immigrant, is beaten near Florence and Normandie.

Federal troops and the California National Guard are mobilized to suppress the riots.

There are requests for emergency responses to more than 140 fires.

Mayor Tom Bradley calls for calm.

April 30

More than forty major fires are still burning out of control.

The US Justice Department announces it will resume its investigation of civil rights violations by the police officers in the King beating.

May 1

Mayor Bradley imposes a dusk-to-dawn curfew.

4,000 National Guardsmen assist police in securing trouble spots in Los Angeles.

National Guard units are federalized by then-President George Bush.

4,000 Army and Marine troops are ordered to act as light infantry and fire if fired upon.

May 4

Relative calm as a majority of rioting ends and damage is assessed.

Upwards of 5,000 people have been arrested.

May 8

The National Guard begins its withdrawal from Los Angeles.

The Crips and Bloods announce a truce.

End Notes

A total of sixty people are dead and 2,383 people are confirmed injured.

A total of 12,545 people have been arrested.

There is an estimated $700 million in property damage and an estimated $1 billion in total damage to the city of Los Angeles.

More than 700 structures have been destroyed by fire.

XII

GEOGRAPHY OF RAGE
Contributors

Pat Alderete

Lisa Alvarez

Teena Apeles
with
Florentino Apeles

Pamela Jo Balluck

Lili Barsha

Anne Beatts

Phillip Brock

Shonda Buchanan

Wanda Coleman

Cara Mia DiMassa

Kitty Felde

Ramón García

Lynell George

Victoria Gutierrez-Kovner

Adolfo Guzman Lopez

Gar Anthony Haywood

Erin Aubry Kaplan

James J. Koch

Larry Kronish

Eric Lax

Peter Maunu

Donna Mungen

Luis Paquime

Kristin L. Petersen

Robert D. Petersen

Gary D. Phillips

Cynthia Adam Prochaska

Renée A. Ruiz

Greg Sarris

Cristián A. Sierra

T. E. Spence

Andrew Tonkovich

David L. Ulin

Marco Villalobos

Oscar Villalon

Scott Wannberg

Ellery Washington C.

Elizabeth Wong

RIOTS

Pat Alderete

My father hated the cops, whether they were sheriff, police, or MP's.

"They're all dogs, mija," he ranted. "You put a badge on a man and he thinks he can do whatever he wants."

"Ay Ernie, my mother pleaded, placing an arm around my brother and me, "you shouldn't teach the children to think like that."

My father shook his head, "You can't put your faith in people who will screw you."

The riot of September 16, 1969 started on the street I grew up on. Tina and I were thirteen years old that autumn. We had grown up next door to each other and, because we fought so much, considered ourselves more like sisters than friends.

We joined the large crowd on Brooklyn Avenue, later to be renamed Avenida Cesar Chavez, to watch the annual parade that celebrated Mexican Independence.

Charros, holding up the flags of both the United States and Mexico, were resplendent in their richly embroidered outfits, riding tall on prancing horses. Politicians with frozen smiles waved lazily from the back seats of convertibles. Rival marching bands from Garfield and Roosevelt High Schools came by in ill-fitting uniforms, each trying to outdo the other on horns and drums.

As the parade continued, the Sheriffs, always a presence at community events and never in groups of less than two, started coming out en masse, dozens of them watching through squinted eyes. The crowd, sensing the tension, grew nervous. A young mother dressed in a china poplana, a regional dress of Southern Mexico festooned with flowers around the rim of the hem, pulled her children roughly towards her, ordering her eldest daughter to hold onto her little sister's hand. An older man, dressed in sweat-stained work clothes, glanced around from under the brim of his worn hat and put his arm protectively around his gray-haired wife.

The group bringing up the end of the procession was the Brown Berets, the Chicano political equivalent of the Black Panthers. To my great joy I saw women marching in their ranks and for the first time in my life I knew what I wanted to be when I grew up. One woman in particular caught my eye. She had shoulder length black hair that curled out from under her beret and framed her face. Though she wasn't especially pretty, I found her beautiful in the way she held herself. She seemed tall in a proud way and her eyes poured fire. She turned and looked directly at me and I wished I had the courage to run beside her.

The Brown Berets were marching in time, led by a pock-faced man in his 30s. They were dressed mostly in army jackets, faded Levis, and boots; they all wore the brown beret. As they walked, the leader shouted, Chicano! and the others would yell Power!, raising their fists in unison. Tina and I thrust our fists skyward.

As they passed the assembled Sheriffs, the leader yelled ¡Marranos! (pigs) as the group rejoined ¡Toma! (take this) and they flipped the Sheriff off.

Tina looked at me and said, "Pata! I can't believe they did that!"

Whoops of gleeful disbelief erupted from the crowd, long-smoldering resentment given voice. People were laughing all around us.

Deep growling from behind me made the hair on the back of my neck stand up. I turned to see a dozen Sheriffs coming our way.

The Sheriffs waded into the crowd, swinging their batons overhead and bringing them down like a rain of hurt. I heard Tina screaming and I turned to see one Sheriff in particular coming our way, his face dripping sweat and twisted with hatred. We ran as tear gas exploded around us and people started choking. I saw the woman in the china poplana dress screaming as her children were separated from her by the confused crowd, the two sisters trying to hang onto each other with both hands. Streams of white smoke streaked all around us, burning our eyes and making us gag.

Tina and I grabbed hands and started running. We hadn't gone far when we were frozen by a new sound. It was the Sheriffs marching down the street. Dozens of heavily booted left feet stomped down, followed by the right foot scraping along the gravel. It was designed to amplify the sound of men marching in the most menacing way possible. Boom scrape, boom scrape. We saw the Sheriff dressed in black riot gear. They held their arms at breast level, holding body-length shields in one hand and batons in the other. Their helmets had thick plastic masks pulled down and covering their chins. A chill ran through me as I realized they were literally dressed to kill.

It was confusing trying to think over the noise of the stomping and the acrid stink of the swirling tear gas. Helicopters swooped low, adding to the roar of screaming and yelling. I could almost feel the low thuds of batons connecting with bodies. Sheriff patrols drove around, some slowly, others darting in and out. Speakers blared, "Get off the streets immediately or face arrest." I couldn't see where anyone could go.

Standing uncertainly in the middle of the street, Tina grabbed at my hand, tears and snot streaming down her face.

Pulling her, I yelled, "We gotta get home!"

We ran up the street, each of us dashing into our own house.

The crowd was running on our lawns and turning on water hoses, desperate for relief from the tear gas. I saw that Joe and Carmen across the street put a bucket of water in their yard. A young man ran to it, dunking his head into it, rubbing furiously at his eyes.

I felt ashamed that I was too scared to help anyone. I cowered behind the living room window, knowing that Tina was doing the same, and I regretted that we had separated. My mom was out on a date with her new boyfriend and I was mad at her for leaving me alone. I curled up into a ball below the window and prayed.

I grew up in East Los Angeles, an unincorporated area that was "served" not by the police but by the Sheriffs Department. Everybody knew they were bullies.

Sometimes at night, a group of Sheriffs would drive through Belvedere Park. Seeing us sitting around, they would flip on their loudspeakers and call out, "Hey you wetbacks, it's late, time to go home. Why don't you swim back to Mexico?"

The fact that most of us were born in the U.S. highlighted the Sheriff's complete and willful ignorance of who we were: native Californians.

When the warfare between varrios reached lethal intensity, the Sheriffs had a game they liked to play. They would pick up a guy from one neighborhood, usually very late at night, and dump him in the middle of enemy territory. They did this to my homeboy Peter when the shit was red hot between Arizona and the Rock. He could have been murdered and the Sheriffs would have considered their hands clean. Everybody knew the Sheriffs did this.

I never felt safe around the Sheriffs. Nobody I knew did.

The August 29, 1970 riots broke out in East Los Angeles during the height of the Chicano Movimiento. The day started peacefully as protestors came together in Laguna Park and marched through East Los Angeles, winding their way down Whittier Boulevard.

In a repeat of the 1969 riot, the Sheriff came down on the marchers, batons beating unprotected bodies, panic spreading through the crowd. The Sheriff used rubber bullets but they didn't bounce harmlessly off people.

Ruben Salazar, a well-respected Chicano journalist, was covering the event for the *Los Angeles Times*. Seeing several Sheriffs heading their way with weapons in hand, he and a group of panicked citizens ran down the street into the Silver Dollar Bar, a tiny watering hole on Whittier Boulevard. As Mr. Salazar looked out the doorway, a

Sheriff took aim with a tear gas rifle and pulled the trigger. The canister struck Mr. Salazar in the head, blowing away a chunk of his skull. He was one of three deaths that day.

I was sickened at the loss of one of the only Chicano role models available. I wished they had instead blown away the Frito Bandito, a big bellied, sombrero wearing gold-toothed fool, probable father to the Taco Bell Chihuahua.

There was an inquiry into Ruben Salazar's death. The Sheriff who pulled the trigger admitted seeing Mr. Salazar look out the doorway but the Sheriff said he feared for his life. The Sheriff had the rifle and Mr. Salazar had a pad and pencil. Nonetheless, following a pattern familiar to my neighborhood, the Sheriff was exonerated. Laguna Park was later renamed Salazar Park, but not many remember who he was.

That the Sheriff was not convicted of wrongdoing proved once again that they had the freedom to do as they wanted with impunity.

The only thing that surprised me about the 1991 Rodney King beating was that people were startled by it. I was grateful it was on videotape. At least, I thought to myself, nobody could deny it. But people could and did. Watching *60 Minutes* on television, Andy Rooney closed the show with the beating. He sat at his desk, bulldog faced as always and said, in his usual tired voice, that nobody showed this part of the tape. The video showed Rodney King shoving the police away before being knocked to the ground and having the shit beat out of him. Andy Rooney came back on and shrugged, as if to imply Mr. King had it coming.

Andy Rooney missed the point. Nobody was saying Rodney King was right. The anger was about the Sheriffs being so casual about brutally beating him, obviously not fearing any kind of reprisal.

I worried when the court venue for the police on trial was changed from Los Angeles to Simi Valley, which has a large percentage of police and sheriffs living there.

My girlfriend at the time, Candy, who was out of work and watching the court proceedings daily, said to me one evening, "You know, Rodney King could have stopped that beating at any time."

"What?" I asked, certain I had misunderstood her.

"Well," she explained, "they played the tape and they showed it in slow motion. You can see when he's on the ground he makes threatening motions. If he had just laid there, they would have stopped beating him."

Anger snaked up my stomach and coiled in my mouth. "Are you stupid? Do you really think anyone would just lay on the ground without moving while they're getting the shit beat out of 'em?"

I felt as if I was looking at Candy from a great distance and there was no getting any closer.

Every day it looked better for the police. I couldn't believe people would think the police were innocently making references to *Gorillas in the Mist*. I remembered the Salazar trial and worried. There seemed an insurmountable gulf between those who knew how common the abuse of power was and those who didn't.

Although I expected the worst, I was still shocked when the not-guilty verdicts were read. During those first critical hours when Los Angeles started to burn, there was not much of a police presence.

By the time the police did come out, events had spiraled and it was too late to stop the outrage. People saw the flames burning out of control but most had failed to see the smoldering embers that had been long in the making. It seemed that people saw the same things very differently.

During the third day of the riots, a news crew was out looking for hope. They were on the street when, improbably, they ran into Huell Howser. Huell Howser, a corny but sweet transplanted Southerner who boasts of California on a local PBS program called *California's Gold*, smiled when the news caster yelped, "Look! It's Huell Howser!"

"So what do you think, Huell? How is your neighborhood doing?"

Huell shook his head and smiled winningly. He said his neighborhood pulled things together and that the situation was much better than how the media was portraying it.

Huell smiled, the newscaster smiled. Meanwhile, a black youth had been standing behind Howser the entire time, on live television, shouting, "Fuck Huell Howser, y'all hear me? Fuck Huell Howser."

PARKER CENTER

Lisa Alvarez

Burning palm trees are spectacular, especially the ones with the absurdly tall, lean trunks that taper near the top into a mop of rustling fronds. When I see them now, these ubiquitous symbols of paradise—of Southern California—I imagine them on fire. I understand how their rustling dried fronds ignite like flammable skirts, how their crowns flame like the pom-poms of an arsonist cheerleader.

I was born in a Los Angeles neighborhood studded with palm trees. West 90th Place and Vermont. 1961. Single-family homes, California bungalows, palms. Look west as you drive the 10 freeway between Century and Manchester and you'll see those trees still. They're closer to the sky now. Some have lost their heads. I admire them most when their lanky forms are silhouetted against the broad sky of a blazing LA sunset. They're silly and majestic at the same time, waving, it seems, to the jets stacked-up and eager to land at LAX.

On the evening of April 29, 1992, I approach a young man carefully pouring gasoline around the trunk of a chubby palm tree in downtown LA. The fuel soaks into the trunk as if the tree is thirsty, and as I watch its callused bark grows dark. The young man is concentrating; the round cheeks of his face are shiny as if he had anointed himself with oil before embarking on his task. But I know it's sweat. My own face is slick too. We are a block or two from Parker Center, LAPD headquarters. It is about 7:30 p.m. The sun is setting. Over half a day has passed since a Simi Valley jury acquitted four police officers charged with beating Rodney King.

At the moment, I am taking a break from the relentless merry-go-round march on the sidewalk outside Parker Center. We have been there since 4:00 p.m., marching, chanting, and eyeing the formidable phalanx of uniformed officers gathered on the lawn as they eye us. We've kept to the sidewalk, walking in a long slow circle. Michael Zinzun, the Pasadena activist who lost an eye in a police beating years earlier, holds a megaphone with one hand and punches at the air with his other. He leads the chant: No Justice, No Peace.

Later that evening, back on the Westside in the subsidized Santa Monica apartment I share with five others, I hear the same reports that everyone did—how the LAPD, usually omnipresent in its black and white cruisers, was missing in action at the areas of severe distress. I can tell you where they all were: surrounding Parker Center. They were, as it's called, protecting their own. I'd never seen so many uniforms in my life.

I am someone who has, at one time or another, described herself as a political activist. I've seen a lot of police. I have attended demonstrations. I've marched, leafleted, gone to jail. I've organized for peace and justice and against poverty and racism. So it seemed natural that, after the announcement of the verdicts, I found myself in one of two cars crammed with my friends, heading eastbound on the 10 toward downtown while the rest of the city, it seemed, was streaming the other way. No second thoughts. We did what we'd done so many times in the past. This was, of course, all coordinated in advance. Community leaders, political and religious, knew that no matter what kind of verdict came down, something needed to happen. People would need a place to speak out, to respond. So the contingency plan. We'd gather at Parker Center, across from City Hall, the headquarters named after William Parker, police chief during the last uprising in LA—Watts—the same police chief who famously and publicly referred to the rioters he faced in 1965 as "monkeys."

Who, exactly, is "we"? The small "we" that huddled in two cars included a social worker, a youth counselor, a legal aid attorney, an urban planner, and the City Attorney of Santa Monica, a man who would be fired a year later for stubbornly refusing to write a law criminalizing homelessness. We are white, black, Latino, working class and middle class, gay and straight. We are friends, but friends in the best sense of the Spanish word, compañeros. Days earlier, on the evening of April 20th, we gathered with hundreds outside the Westside Federal Building to protest resumption of the death penalty and the execution of Robert Alton Harris. The "we" who assembles at Parker Center includes local community leaders and people who I have seen for years at one demonstration and another. As we circle, I recognize their faces. We have done this before. Others are present too and I suspect that for some, this is their first such activity. Their outrage at the verdicts has led them where their pastor, priest, rabbi, friend, or neighbor has pointed and they find themselves, perhaps for the first time, exercising their Constitutional rights to assemble freely and express themselves. By sunset, the few hundred who first assembled have grown to over a thousand.

Earlier, the network TV vans arrived and the crews dutifully filmed our march. But they seemed disinterested, distracted. Indeed, the open doors of the vans revealed live feeds from other sites in the city. We gathered along with the crews to watch the bank of tiny monitors, spread out not unlike the bright blue squares of television's Jeopardy game show. I'll take Police Abuse for two hundred, Alex. Urban Unrest for a thousand. Today is a Daily Double, for sure.

There, peering into the van's interior, I see raw footage of fires and looting, watch the tape loop of the beating of another man near Florence and Normandie, trucker Reginald Denny, and hear about his rescue. Until then I don't know, as many around me do not, that the city isn't quiet, that people aren't settling down to another evening of reruns and rented videos after watching the evening news which leads, of course, with the verdicts.

The seasoned discipline that the crowd exercised earlier begins to deteriorate as the numbers grow and night begins to fall. The footage from the vans causes some to leave and others to stay. On the traffic island in the middle of Los Angeles Street, my friends and I consult each other. At the insistence of our friend, City Attorney Bob, we agree to stay a little longer, hoping to help ward off the violence like that we witnessed on the TV monitors. I don't believe this is possible. While some still march, much of the crowd masses in one place, facing off with the cops. There's a sense that something could rip or tear open. I walk away to get some air, to calm myself and that's when I meet the young man who wants to burn palm trees.

He carries a bright red plastic fuel can, the kind you buy at gas stations for cheap when your car conks out a few blocks away. He applies the gasoline almost lovingly to the tree, as if it is food or medicine.

Now I can see the clouds of the new night sky are illuminated not by the residue of a setting sun, but by faraway and nearby fires. The young man in front of me wedges newspaper into the cut fronds of the palm tree that form part of its trunk. He reaches for matches.

"Don't," I ask him. "Please." My voice sounds funny, small, cracked.

He looks at me as if I am crazy. "Why not?" he asks.

"It's a tree," I say. "It didn't do anything. It's just a tree." I feel foolish, ashamed for worrying about a palm tree.

"Listen, lady," he says, leaning close. "It's not a real tree. It's a fake one. They're all fake." He swings his arms toward the city trees that stand at attention in their little plots of dirt. "They shouldn't be here. I'm taking this one out. Don't worry. It'll be all right."

He lights his newspaper and fire flames up the trunk like the backyard barbecues that, as a child, I drenched in lighter fluid. The tree will burn for a good long time. I move away but out of habit, I put my hands palms up, toward the fire, as if to gather the heat in, as if it is a campfire and not a burning palm tree.

"See," the young man tells me as he caps his gas can, "I told you it wasn't real. If it was real, it wouldn't burn. What's real doesn't burn." His logic seems to please him. He flashes me a smile and I realize just how young he is. I'm thirty-one. He's young. Sixteen. Fifteen. He's a kid.

I rejoin the crowd at Parker Center just in time to witness a scene that I'll see televised repeatedly in the coming days. Since the fortress of Parker Center is, for the most part, impenetrable, some in the crowd search for elements that are not. Specifically, the guard booth that regulates access to the employee parking lot attracts their attention. It's small. It's unoccupied. It's built of wood and glass. It takes a few people, but not many, to topple it, and once it's on its side, all it requires is a couple of young men with gas canisters and matches. Someone adds an American flag to the mini-conflagration. Many in the crowd roar their approval while others try to remove the flag. I return to the cement traffic island, hoping to find my friends, hoping to go home, hoping the street and the island will act as some kind of buffer zone. It seems to. Los Angeles Street remains empty. The crowd surges toward Parker Center, toward the phalanx of the police who have stood so long, it seems, at attention.

I watch as the air fills with rocks, plants, shoes, pieces of wood, and the contents of trash cans. It's a storm of debris, run-off, cast-offs. Later my friend Anne tells me that at this point she thought we were going to be shot. She separates from the crowd and, like me, tries to find her friends in the melee. Instead she bumps into a kid, maybe sixteen, with a huge rock in his hand. It's obvious he plans to lob it at the cops. Anne, a youth counselor, tries then and there to counsel the kid. She begs him not to throw it, to calm down. She tells him that she thinks his life might be in danger. He ignores her and chucks the rock—and then picks up another. She remembers feeling like a baby that night, thinking that all these years she had only been playing around at politics and that when it came down to it she didn't know anything about that kid's life and what gave his young eyes the look of complete abandon as he threw one rock and then another and then another.

On the traffic island I discover that, by hugging a utility box, I can stay put while the crowd, rebuffed by the now advancing police, surges back, crossing Los Angeles Street toward City Hall. Within minutes, the police have successfully pushed back the crowd with shields and batons, guns still undrawn. They've taken back the lawn of Parker Center and most of the sidewalk. This leaves the crowd without a clear target. Some turn to parked vehicles, easily enough overturned. Others break into small groups and set out in various directions. But some advance with determination on a building adjacent to City Hall. To this day, I still don't understand why they didn't advance on City Hall itself. The group, moving now like a single entity, turned its attention on this nearby building.

I recognize it. The Children's Museum. A woman breaks apart from the group and runs ahead. She leaps up the steps. She faces them and shouts, "You don't want to hurt this place. This is a good place. This is the Children's Museum." She stares them all down.

"Now," she says, "the *L.A. Times* is right down the street." She points vaguely to the right, her long skinny arm like an arrow. "I suggest you go there."

The group seems to follow her suggestion and troops, almost as one, down in the direction of Times Mirror Square. If I had a voice like the woman on the museum steps, perhaps I would have told them to give it up, warned them that the Times building had been dynamited over eighty years earlier by militant trade unionists trying to strike a blow against the despotic General Otis and his anti-labor policies. The rebuilt building was purposefully designed to resist attacks. But I don't say a thing. I hug my utility box and remember the doomed McNamara brothers and wonder where my friends are. As the crowd thins out, I notice I have company. Journalist Mike Davis scribbles nearby on a notepad, his crew-cut head bent low. Days later I'll read his account in the *L.A. Weekly*.

My friends re-appear. We decide, with little discussion, to leave. More trees have ignited. Cars are turned over and torched. We had parked near St. Vibiana's Cathedral, soon to be damaged in the Northridge quake, and then abandoned. The cathedral is dark, ghostly. Its surrounding sidewalks are resting places for the homeless. I know this well, and yet that evening, to walk a couple blocks and turn the corner and find the long line of restless sleepers stretched out, just minutes away from the flames and unrest is startling. Of course the homeless would be here. Where else would they go? Much has changed in the last few hours, but not this. Men and women still sleep on the streets of Los Angeles, even in a riot.

We walk past in silence. They sleep, already having slid into makeshift cardboard sleeping quarters, heads resting on backpacks, nearby shopping carts filled with possessions. This is one night when the police will not hassle them.

In our cars, heading west on the deserted 10 freeway, we see fires to the south and some to the north. I think of the kid lighting palm trees and his conviction that what's real doesn't burn.

My friend Anne puts something in my hand. "I found it," she says. "It was just lying there in the grass. So I picked it up."

It's cold and heavy. It's the metal letter "C" from Parker Center.

THE GETAWAY

Teena Apeles with Florentino Apeles

One of my worst nightmares is to know when my parents' lives are in danger. When I heard of the beginnings of what became one of the most violent days in Los Angeles' history, I was an hour away in Orange County watching a live newscast. The television showed a Caucasian man being pulled out of a truck and beaten around Florence and Normandie, just miles away from my dad's gas station. News reports relayed other incidents of racial conflict in which Korean businesses, and persons who looked Korean or Asian, were being targeted as well. I immediately called my father on his cell, telling him what was happening. "It's headed your way Dad!"

I was pleading with him to go home and close the gas station at Normandie, the same place that, less than a year before, my mother was pistol-whipped by an African-American male who then stole her car. My dad laughed at me, claiming everything would be fine. But there had been existing racial/economic tension for years in that area of town between the predominantly African-American residents and occupying Korean—in my dad's case, Filipino—business owners.

Despite my begging he wouldn't listen, and I hung up the phone only to pray for my dad's safety as newscasts on every channel showed violence and looting edging closer and closer to his destination.

Soon after, my father received another call that echoed my concerns. He recalls the events as such:

"I was driving south on the Harbor Freeway when I got a call from my cashier, Danny, at our Normandie and 23rd GasMart. He asked if he could close the station. It was about 6:00 p.m. He heard the news on the radio and television that the 'mob' was heading north. I asked him to wait for me so my architect friend (who was in the car with me at that time) and I could help him close since we were still near by.

"Five minutes after our arrival at the station, Danny yelled that the mob was coming. My friend and I were in the back office preparing to lock up. I was about to step into the store to check it out when my friend, who was trembling from fear, held me back. 'You're crazy to go out!'

"We could hear people hollering. We locked the office door and climbed atop our filing cabinet to get to the attic and hid there in the cramped space while the mob vandalized and ransacked the mini mart. After an hour, when the noise subsided and the 'coast was clear,' we rushed out and got into my now-battered car—all the upholstery was torn up, the stereo was ripped out, and every window was shattered—both of us sitting on the broken glass.

"As we were leaving the mob returned. Men were rushing in front of my car with a hail of rocks. I had to hit two guys with my bumper that tried to come after us, blocking our escape. Thankfully we were able to get out…the rioters tried to run after us for a block, up to the freeway ramp.

"The Santa Monica (10) Freeway East/Harbor (110) Freeway was empty that early evening. We abandoned the station to the mob. My cashier, Danny, fled as the rioters came, though they did not harm him since they said he was "Latino" and he didn't bother to fight them for fear for his life.

"Rioters grabbed whatever they could—cash box, cigarettes, merchandise, etc. They smashed up the windows, and even tried to set the station on fire. The next day our local window washers who we had befriended over the years, James and his wife (both African-American), told us they were able to stop the rioters from setting our business aflame."

"The rioters caused some $35K damage/loss to our gas station, not including the damage to my car."

It turned out my father's business was one of the few "Korean"-owned gas stations that didn't burn to the ground in the area. I was still behind the Orange Curtain when I called my parents that next morning. And guess where they were? Back at the station, cleaning up the aftermath, completely in denial that people were still rioting throughout the city. This time I spoke to my mom who said, "Don't worry dear, we're okay here."

The violence and looting continued for a few days before I drove out to see my parents, who have only fully relayed the details of my father's getaway nearly a decade after the event. In asking my parents to tell their side of the story via email, my mom began her story with "Here's what Dad dictated to me:" ending the account with, "It was a terrifying experience. Thank God we lived to tell about it!!"

Today, they still own and operate the Normandie gas station, despite my sisters and me asking them to sell it after my mother was first car jacked. My parents would simply respond, "It's our most profitable business; it paid for your college education."

Yet I constantly wonder, at what cost? My sisters and I are well out of college now, but just recently, at another business, this time a car wash/gas station off the 10 freeway at National and Robertson, my parents were held up again at gunpoint. Thankfully, their lives were spared on this occasion as well. It's sometimes hard for me to discern if it is my parents' choice of businesses off that damned 10 Freeway or being Filipino or the city of Los Angeles or the acquittal of the police officers who brutally beat Rodney King that really put my parents' lives at stake.

Regardless, how long before my parents' escape routes come to a close? If the experience during the LA Riots wasn't enough to scare them, what will?

MANIFESTATION

Lili Barsha   17

Am temping at the accounting firm of Feinstein and Rosengold when Rosengold calls me into Feinstein's office and points to the television set.

"Look, your neighborhood's on fire," says Rosengold.

Indeed, pictures of Koreatown in flames, men with shotguns on roof-tops, smoke billowing from the corner where I live.

Leave Santa Monica to return home and protect my cat, Bob.

On the way home radio reports freeway closings. Am driving Butterscotch, a 1984 Dodge Omni, so named for its color. Exit at La Brea instead of Western, which is sealed off. At Venice Boulevard a man at a gas station waves a gun in the air. Another man with a sawed-off rifle stands at the next gas station. All the guns I've seen in my life, I see on this day.

While stopped at a red light near Pico, a Volkswagen bug driven by a woman pulls up next to me. A guy with a baseball bat gets out, smashes the window of the car in front of me and punches the driver. I start to cry in empathy for the driver and inadvertently make eye contact with the man with the baseball bat.

"What are you crying at?" he asks. "Want me to give you something to cry about?" I decline.

The man with the bat and his girlfriend speed away. La Brea becomes a freeway. Every witness to the scene drives without regard to traffic signals. The point becomes not stopping.

I reach home and am greeted by a man in front of my apartment building loading the trunk of his car with pilfered Pringles potato chips.

"Big party!" he shouts.

Watch from my living room window on First Street as men rush home from Vermont Avenue with stolen television sets, and women hurry back with stolen diapers.

Decide to take pictures and win Pulitzer prize in photography but camera is snatched out of my hands by passer-by as I exit the building.

Return to living room. Bob and I listen to "Burnin' and Lootin' " by Bob Marley.

During curfew to come, topped off by stationing of National Guardsmen at Ralph's Supermarket, am chastised by friends and family for finding inappropriate humor in leaving the following message on my answering machine:

"I'm out looting, can't come to the phone right now."

MONTANA BURNS!

Anne Beatts

I was working at a job I hated, with people I hated. We were writing a network TV pilot. My co-workers were nice middle-class straight white guys. They were also racist and sexist. When I suggested that we add a black character to the cast, one of them took that as a cue to ask me, "Have you ever fucked a black guy?"

That's why the headline in the ad jumped out at me: "Theatre in the Last Best Place." I decided to quit my job and go to Montana. I'd take my TV network blood money and spend it on a week-long theatre workshop in Big Fork, Montana.

Now that I was going, the TV people wanted me to stay. For the first time the producer asked for my opinion of the latest rewrite. I told him I was leaving for Montana the next day but agreed to give him my notes. I was finishing them up when I heard the verdict on the radio news. I knew it meant trouble. A friend came over and we watched the uprising on TV while I packed. My planned escape to Montana was my own personal uprising, a revolt against the system that was stifling my creativity. I wasn't going to let anything interfere with it. Not even a city in flames.

Next morning, my flight was cancelled. I booked another one

from Burbank that got cancelled too. Finally I decided I would just go to the airport. It was about 4:00 p.m. I called a car service. The driver, a white ex-cop, took the long way from Hollywood to LAX through the deserted streets of Beverly Hills. In Culver City, we passed a flaming 7-11, also deserted.

At the airport they told me to go home and observe the curfew. I refused. I asked to speak to a supervisor. I was determined to get on a plane, any plane. Finally they said I could get on a jumbo jet, too big to be re-routed to Burbank or John Wayne Airport, that was coming in from Hawaii at 10:00 p.m. and heading on to Salt Lake City. I could spend the night there and make it to Montana in the morning.

As we flew over downtown LA we could see the smoke and flames. In Salt Lake, I shared a ride to the hotel with a pilot who explained why Utah didn't have a race problem like LA's: "We never let them in."

When I finally got to Big Fork, it looked like paradise: a one-street old-fashioned town on a lake tucked beneath snow-capped mountains. People either pressed me for news of the "riots" or delicately avoided the subject. It was hard to get information. The lakeshore motel had no CNN. By the time *USA Today* arrived in Big Fork it was USA Yesterday.

The radio carried the news of looting on Hollywood Boulevard, a stone's throw from my apartment. My cat-sitter told me over the phone that neighborhood vigilantes had created a barricade at the end of my street, and that they had guns. I told him to help himself to the frozen spaghetti sauce in my fridge. It was very strange being in paradise talking about art while Los Angeles burned.

In class we each had to write a ten-minute play. I decided to write about the destruction I wasn't witnessing. I imagined the looting of Frederick's of Hollywood. An exotic dancer and a black transvestite get caught in the act by a white rookie cop, and eventually escape by invoking Madonna's help. The play was called "Divine Intervention."

There was one African-American student in the workshop. I cornered him in the town's one bar and he agreed to be in my play. The reading was a big success.

When I got back from Big Fork, LA was scarred, but still there. My writer friend Meri Danquah called me and said that someone was putting an anthology together to commemorate the uprising, and did I have anything to contribute? "Well," I said, "I have this play…" They published it.

Next April, someone called and said that they were putting together a benefit performance evening at Atlas, and did I have anything? "Well," I said, "I have this play…"

I managed to obtain an authentic LAPD uniform and a starter pistol for the actor who played the cop. There was a rumor that "certain elements" were planning to impersonate LAPD officers during possible "repeat riots" on the impending anniversary of Rodney King. I didn't want to have to account for the uniform and gun in my trunk. So I drove very carefully on the way to Atlas the day of the dress rehearsal.

Later that afternoon at Atlas, we were in mid-rehearsal when suddenly the empty restaurant was filled with real cops. Apparently a passer-by, looking in through the window, had seen a cop struggling with a black man inside the restaurant and had reacted by calling 911. It took a lot of explaining to get the LAPD to leave. We offered them free tickets to the performance, but they didn't show.

On the anniversary of the Rodney King verdict, the city failed to burn a second time.

THE LAST BLOND BIMBO IN NEW YORK CITY

Phillip Brock

"Just the champagne?"

3:00 p.m., Thursday, April 30, 1992; express check out, Pavilion's market, Ventura Boulevard, Sherman Oaks, California; the end of the world as we know it. And I feel fine.

"Yeah, thanks. Oh—and the flowers, too. Thanks."

I swear I hear the checker mutter "Great…" as he grabs the intercom mike and calls out "Price check on some flowers…"

Kim, my girlfriend of five months, a lovely, gifted, and quite sexy actress approaching forty, had spent all of pilot season asking for and receiving my reassurance that she is indeed still lovely, gifted, and quite sexy, and that she has every reason to believe in a beneficent universe. And what do you know—it worked! She booked a pilot—one of the last pilots to be cast that season. Even though I'd given up drink a year earlier, I thought it'd be a nice gesture to buy her some champagne and get myself out to Venice where she lived to celebrate; a struggle for some familiarity in a world gone suddenly topsy-turvy. It was such a relief to be able to celebrate a victory instead of the seemingly endless line of defeats this town metes out to most of its actors every spring. Just a free and clear hooray! Except for that pesky Simi Valley thing.

Bang! Bang Bang! I look back over my shoulder to see where the sound is coming from. Some hapless woman has bottlenecked two food and diaper laden carts into a gap between the magazine stand and the produce, and a seventysomething man in Snoopy-pattern golf pants is systematically backing his cart up and ramming it into hers, trying to dislodge her, as if she'd just blocked the last road out and Godzilla was in town.

I was still an actor then, living in a little back house on Fredonia Drive in Studio City. An hour earlier, this second day of the riots, after I'd had a night and half the next day for it to sink in that the verdicts hadn't been a mistake, I'd been down in my place watching it all on the news. Samy's, the huge camera place on Beverly, had just been set ablaze. Why Samy's? I thought. What could anyone have against a camera shop? I felt more terrified and lonesome than I had been in my entire life. kept trying to call my parents back in Oklahoma, but I couldn't get a line out. The night before, my mom had called and told me to carry a copy of *The Nation* with me, in case I got dragged out of my car, I could hold it up and cry, "I'm on your side!" She'd seen what had happened to Reginald Denny.

Two huge blasts suddenly reverberated off of the walls outside my house. All right, I told myself, the gardener's old pick-up back-fires like that sometimes. Cars backfire all the time. Or, someone could have hurled a stick of dynamite out of a passing vehicle. That happens sometimes too.

The manager has approached. The checker holds up the bunch of flowers like it's the actual fiddle Nero played while Rome burned.

"How much for these?" he asks.

"And *The Nation*?" I ask, "Do you carry *The Nation*? A magazine?"

"I don't know, sir, you'd have to go look in the magazines."

"Oh, that's all right," I say as the line behind me grows audibly impatient.

After I thought it was safe to stop cowering in the shower, I decided to see what the hell had made those blasts.

As I crawled up to the street, I heard the bougainvillea in front of the house next door rustling, and my neighbor Schroder stepped out to greet me. He held a shot gun in his hands, what looked to be a 16 gauge. I smiled, friendly, neighborly. Schroder was a sixty-year-old retired high-school auto shop teacher who lived alone in his boyhood home. Just Schroder, his Doberman, an eight-foot-long boa constrictor, and some definite ideas about what had transpired in the time leading up to and since the Rodney King beating.

"What were those gunshots?" I asked.

"That was me."

"What the hell happened?"

"A carload of blacks drove past three times in fifteen minutes," he said, and now I think I'm beginning to hear faint traces of an Afrikaans accent.

"Schroder—Jesus—maybe they're lost—"

"I fired a couple of rounds off just to let them know we're ready."

"Ready? Well...I'm not ready! I'm not ready at all! If you pissed them off, what am I gonna do? You think some Beach Boys records at full blast might scare 'em off? 'Cause that's about all I've got. Christ," I shook my head and started to walk back to my place. Schroder called out after me.

"I don't care what the video looks like, the jury was right—policemen have to take precautions! PCP is so contagious that if Rodney King had been on PCP, an officer could get high just from touching him with his bare hands!"

I pictured a chain of cops, one hand on the shoulder of the officer in front of them, all standing frozen, smiling, suddenly realizing they are Gods Who Can Fly, and Rodney's PCP engorged body lying on the ground as the conduit at the head of the chain, like the Brothers Grimm fairy tale of the goose who laid the golden egg.

"So, what," I said, "is the paint on the nightstick PCP resistant or something? Keeps it from crawling up their sleeves?"

A fight has broken out in aisle five over the last remaining bottles of Gerber's. The store is packed to the gills with panicked shoppers sliding armloads of nibblets and canned hash and flashlight batteries off the quickly emptying shelves into quickly filling baskets.

I reach for my wallet and give what I hope looks like a "we're all in this together" wink to the checker. The African-American checker. The Checker of Color. Who is now glaring at me. I'm not being paranoid. I know he is glaring.

"Ooo-kaaay," he says, "just the champagne and flowers." As he bags the two bottles, I think that he's imagining me later this evening, calling out to my blond cheerleader of a wife back in my cozy, gated domicile, a glass of sparkling wine in hand, sitting in front of my wide screen: "Honey—will you stop warming the brie for five seconds and come look—they're burning another Korean deli!"

Back down in my apartment, the phone rang and it was my girlfriend Kim, screaming Oh Jesus, now what?

"I got it!"

"Are you okay?"

"I got it!"

"Got what?"

"Well, duh—the part! Thirteen guaranteed episodes on air! Nicolletta's on the phone with them now arguing about my hair. I'm playing the last blond bimbo in New York City, can you stand it? Uh-ha-ha-hAAAH! I wonder if I'll have to dye it or if they'll use a wig..."

"Unbelievable."

"Right? They're meeting my quote, that's what was holding them up the whole time. Apparently, the producers loved me, it was just—"

"So, listen—Kim—I want to come over, can I come over? I don't want to be alone."

"I know—yuck, huh? About everything? On TV?"

"Can I come over?"

"Sure. Only be careful. There's a curfew and I hear traffic is moida. Wup—that's me, I should take it."

"See you soon."

"Mmmwwwah."

"I—"

But she'd clicked over already.

For a rebellious instant, I almost ask the checker—"Ooh, do you guys carry Beluga?" But then I look back again through the line of shoppers who've completely disregarded the "12 items or less" sign. At this point I'm seriously doubting my fellow Angeleno's sense of noblesse, so I pay up and head for the parking lot.

Traffic isn't so bad inching out of Pavillion's, but just after I pull onto the upgrade from the Valley over Beverly Glen, it starts getting weird. Three pick-ups come streaming by in a row, downhill from town into the Valley, all loaded with white boys, all with huge American flags flying and Lynard Skynard tunes blazing which strikes me as, in context, a bit brazen. I have to fight off the urge to crack a bottle of the champagne, turn around, head back to my suddenly cozy seeming hovel, and pull the covers around my head until this thing blows over.

When I finally crest Mulholland drive, I see the fires burning here and there all over the flats, some flames high enough to be seen at the ocean. The good dozen pillars of smoke and fire scattered around the basin look like points on a connect the dots playbook, and the picture that forms in the sky spells out RAGE, pure and simple.

And then I am plunged down into the south slope of Beverly Glen leading into Bel-Air, where no fires rage at all. Actually, with the exception of the crawling traffic, I'd never know that we are a convoy of rather petty refugees.

From the distance of years, I'm surprised at how few things I remember about the drive to Kim's. I felt so panicked and out of control that day, but the things I recall seem rather mundane: a "Baby on Board" sticker in the rear window of the SUV in front of me that seemed to be as sad a plea for mercy as my mother's suggestion that I carry a copy of *The Nation*; a stunningly wrong turn I made off Sunset in Brentwood, where I had to drive five miles out of my way through one of those "if you're lost, you don't belong here" type of neighborhoods, just to make a right turn back into the flow of traffic I'd pulled out of to make my attempt at a shortcut in the first place; and the sense that my VW convertible now felt not so much like California de-riguer as a motorcar carrying a rather unpopular figure through the streets of a war zone.

I can't believe how happy I am to see Kim's bungalow off one of the walk streets just west of Lincoln. The trip from my house to hers, which normally takes thirty minutes tops, has taken me three and a half hours.

Kim opens the door with a phone to her ear, looking past my right shoulder.

"Thirteen guaranteed episodes on air! Nicolletta's on the phone with them now arguing about my hair."

"Oh…my…god…" I say, holding up my champagne bottles and flowers with a look on my face that I hope bears the full import of the drive I've just made.

Kim turns away and walks back into the house.

"I'm playing the last blond bimbo in New York City, can you stand it? Uh-ha-ha-hAAAH! I wonder if I'll have to dye it or if they'll use a wig…"

I look over my right shoulder to see what Kim was gazing at so intently, but nothing is there. I step inside the house and close and lock and dead bolt the door.

"Right? They're meeting my quote, that's what was holding them up the whole time. Apparently, the producers loved me, it was just the network trying to figure out—yeah, well, you know I read for them last year."

Suddenly Kim seems to notice me. Her face brightens and she smiles and skips across the room. She gives me a kiss on the cheek and squeezes my shoulder and mouths, "Can you believe it?!"

"I know," she says, back into the phone, "yuck, huh? About every-thing? On TV? There's a curfew and I hear traffic is moida. Wup— that's me, I should take it. Okay. Mmmwwwah!"

I step into the kitchen and start to look for an ice bucket. I know she has one somewhere, because I'd bought her a bottle of cham-pagne for Valentine's day. I locate it in the rear of the cupboard beneath the sink and am just reaching for it when I hear her scream-ing from the den. I nail the back of my head as I stand and rush in to see if anything new has happened on the television which is on and muted in a corner of the room.

Kim stands with the phone to her ear, watching the silent screen.

"I got it! I got it! Well, duh—the part! Thirteen guaranteed episodes on air! Nicolletta's on the phone with them now arguing about my hair. I'm playing the last blond bimbo in New York City, can you stand it? Uh-ha-ha-hAAAH! I wonder if I'll have to dye it or if they'll use a wig..."

She turns to me and starts gesturing towards the screen. I walk over to her, rubbing the back of my head.

"Isn't she amazing?" she stage whispers to me. "That newsperson, Jodi Baskerville? She's going to be huge after this. She is hot..."

She starts walking away from me toward the kitchen.

"They're meeting my quote, that's what was holding them up the whole time. Apparently, the producers loved me, it was just the network trying to figure out—yeah, well, you know I read for them last year."

I sit down on the couch and start watching the city burn. It takes on a whole other tone after night falls. A transformer on La Brea has just exploded. Neighbors, young people of all different colors are trying to put out fires, confronting looters. As I watch the tube, I hear the growing drone of a helicopter until it sounds like it's right over our house. As if on cue, the television image shifts to Lincoln Boulevard in Venice. A Kragen Auto Parts store just around the corner has been ransacked and set on fire. The helicopter sounds like it's trying to land on our bungalow.

"I know!" Kim stands in the kitchen, emptying a tray into the ice bucket with one hand, covering her ear with the other and yelling into the phone, "yuck, huh? About everything? On TV? There's a curfew and I hear traffic is moida! Wup—that's me, I should take it. Okay. Mmmwwwah!"

Police sirens are now screaming up Lincoln, the Sensaround soundtrack to the muted image I'm watching on the television.

"Honey," I say, "you might want to come see this. They've set fire to a store right around the corner..."

From the linen closet at the far end of the kitchen, I hear Kim's muffled screams.

"Honey—Jesus!" I stand up and storm into the kitchen. "Will you put down the damn phone for five—" but she can't hear me. Her muffled voice knocks up against the door from inside the linen closet, where she's retreated for some quiet. I stand there looking at the kitchen counter, at the two bottles of champagne, one with the foil thingy unwrapped, but still corked. But still corked. But still corked. Some one needs to drink this, I think. She must see that. Somebody in this house needs to be drinking right now. As I pop the cork, grab a glass and begin to pour, the door to the linen closet opens. I turn, caught. Saved? Caught. No, saved.

"Yeah, I'm watching it now. Isn't she amazing, Jodi Baskerville? She's going to be huge after this. She is hot—yeah—right?"

She crosses to her purse as she speaks, lights a cigarette, then crosses back to the linen closet, taking the glass of champagne from my hand, mouthing the words, "Thank you!" as she does.

"They're meeting my quote, that's what was holding them up the whole time. Apparently, the producers loved me…" and then she's back in the linen closet and the muffled voice again.

I've come to understand that she could no more have hung up her phone that night than I could have strolled up the street to the 7-11 for a Big Gulp. We do what we do to feel safe. Back then I wasn't really a man who could be too solidly leaned upon….

I think of driving back to Studio City, then the fires and police all over Lincoln Boulevard make me realize that as separate as I feel from my girlfriend right now, at least bullets aren't whizzing past my head on either side. I make a bowl of microwave popcorn, move to the couch, put the blanket over my legs and stare at the television.

It wasn't until years later that we both put it together that we didn't break up because I was intimidated by her success.

Kim leaves the linen closet screaming, grabs the open bottle from the counter, and passes through the den "…well, duh—the part!" and goes out into the backyard, still holding the phone to her ear. I turn and look at her, lovely Kim, through the sliding glass doors, staring at the night sky, as happy as I've ever seen her. And I wonder, if I leave her tonight, if I end this thing now, will it destroy her performance in the pilot? Or if I stay until she's done filming, am I a coward pretending to care? What's the "good guy" thing to do? I haven't been schooled in the "when the world falls apart" etiquette.

I turn back to the TV I think I hear a vague "Uh-ha-ha-hAAAH!" from outside, but it could just be the rotor blades on the chopper that still hovers over Kragen Auto Parts.

32

MIDNIGHT CRY:
In Leimert Park The Question Isn't About The Verdicts

Shonda Buchanan

Two days before the verdicts, I pretended to be deaf and blind. I willed my fingers to forget how to write, despising my desire to record images and my link with the vultures hovering over South Central, picking our bones for front-page news. I tried to seek strength in silence. But so many black people have died tongueless, unable to utter a word. My mind was frozen on the possibility of exoneration for the four police officers. Images of black, dickless bodies dangling from oak trees kept flashing behind my eyelids. The cops simply couldn't go free.

It's fatigue that engulfs us—fatigue over King, Latasha Harlins, Oliver Beasley, Huey Newton. We are tired of the fear and the hopeless, instantaneous rage that erupts from our collective consciousness. Tired of sending the children to bed early so they won't see the tears. I know other midnight criers by the tightness of their lips and harsh gazes. But no, they will not make me cry, not again, not this time. Since the verdicts, my sobs are pent up in my chest, held back from their natural flow by man-made traps. Beneath the veneer of the "favorable" verdicts, and the immense sigh of relief oozing from every crevice in LA, there is still the question of the future. What happens when the sentencing comes for Koon and

Powell? And will the LA3 get a fair trail? And can we really just all get along? Beneath the "peace" that seems to be suffusing the city, there is a history of disappointment and the potential for disaster. Was this really a victory?

While a "love your neighbor" attitude was being promoted at middle-class black congregations, on the Wednesday before the verdicts white citizens were arming themselves against a "reaction" from the "hood dwellers" to the American justice system. The alienation of white and black suburbia from the inner city combined with the doublespeak of politicians and the media has always hindered a togetherness attitude. Or, in lay terms, the white man will fuck a nigga in the ass every chance he gets—dry, with no Vaseline.

Let's take it to the streets. Leimert Park, one week before verdict deliberations: On Thursday night, Coltrane is flowing over the speakers downstairs while upstairs at 5th Street Dicks, a jazz/coffee house, a poetry reading is raging. The owner, Richard Fullerton, has confidence that if anything goes down, his place would be left alone. "I don't think they had any intention of destroying black businesses last year," he says. "If we don't get it right there's going to be an explosion. Black people have a right to be angry. I hope there is justice, but I don't believe in the system anyway."

5th Street Dicks opened two days before last year's Rebellion; they've been serving up cappuccino and mocha java since. Sara Wright, a regular patron of the club, sits at the counter sipping coffee. "Those four officers should be tried and put in the penitentiary," she says. "Not under supervision, but with everybody else in the yard. See if they like it."

On Saturday before Easter Sunday, 43rd and Degnan is alive with artists, dancers, and a full-blown jam session inside the World Stage, a small studio that serves as a jazz fix for old and young cats. Down the street, Museum in Black holds one of the largest collection of African Art in LA. Collector/owner Brian Breye is concerned about the militaristic strategy of the LAPD. "The police department needs to take a better view of public relations," says Breye. "They have a tendency to create psychological intimidation. The police department, at the rate they are going, is creating a police state."

Back across the street, Earl Underwood, of Black & Gold African Statuary, relaxes in the sun. "We might have learned something as a people past time. We reacted out of blind rage. It will be more of a direction with the rage this time. It will be more focused towards the oppressive forces." As if on cue, police and ambulance sirens punctuate his voice.

April 17, Saturday morning, 6:36 sat like salt on my tail. A gray fog of silence settled on the "Jungle," a term for the labyrinth of apartment projects off of Coliseum Avenue where I live. When the verdicts were read, people gave a collective holler, "Yes!" The newscasters were not required to put on the pensive frown for the moment.

In Leimert Park, Sara Wright is at 5th Street Dicks, sounding optimistic. "The white man is embarrassed by this," she says. "This is the first criminal case in American history that white men have been tried and convicted for beating a black man, but your generation feels differently," she adds slowly, noticing my hesitation to agree. "The significance of this case is big when you look at the history of black folks—when white men would cut black men's balls off and stuff 'em down they throat."

But those who sense a change in LA must have a sixth sense because on TV, I see Korean and white shop owners with guns ready to use against black youth. I see black youth seething with a 400-year-old anger and frustration supposedly aimed at the "white establishment" but that inevitably destroys themselves. I see Latinos, African-Americans, Asians all scrambling for the tiniest slice of economic pie in one of the richest cities in the world.

With the apparent release of tension I bet the city and its "leaders" must feel pretty stupid. The lack of faith in themselves and the system they work for speaks to their inadequacy to govern. The show of brute force by Willie [Williams] and friends proved to some in the black community that he learned in the black community that he learned his lessons in Philly—where cops firebombed MOVE's complex—real well. And Uncle Tom Bradley told us good. "Ya'll bet not think of trying anything or massa's gon' be real angry." Shuffle, scuff. One could ask Willie and Tom how they felt protecting Angelenos and their property from people who look just like them.

The question of the future still rides me like a bad fuck. I just hope black people aren't the last to know that their civil rights have been sacrificed to all the televised good faith and prayers for a united LA. Maybe, just maybe, the grind of the justice system is beginning to shift gears to include us and not crush us beneath its wheel. Otherwise all is for naught and our cries and Christian prayers will go unheard—again.

THE RIOT INSIDE ME: A STATISTIC SPEAKS

Wanda Coleman

Each time I think back on the summer of 1992, my head and heart ache. I am as reluctant as ever to write personally about the violence protesting the verdict in the Rodney King beating case. I took one opportunity when I guest-edited a special issue of High Performance magazine—an independent effort that went unnoticed outside Los Angeles. Rhetoric comes easily when speaking of 'the issues,' as I did—or attempted to do—at the forums, panels, and town meetings that occurred in the wake of the South Central Riots, the largest man-made destruction in the history of 20th Century U.S.A. I am calling them riots because that is what they were. I have exhausted the politically correct jargon of rebellion or insurrection. As I was a witness, people—of nearly every ethnic description—were in the streets smiling as they looted. It wasn't going to be just a Black affair that time around, not the way it was when Watts burned twenty-seven years earlier. I did not engage in the looting myself—not in 1965 and not in 1992. For me, the fact that others were so engaged was spectacle enough. Long after the flames died and curfew lifted, the riot inside me waged on.

It had been ignited three months before April 29th by a failed job interview. I drove the streets fiercely, struck the steering wheel, and cried profanities aloud. The hissy far transcended the incident that triggered it. I did not know it at the time, but my systemic hypotension was becoming hypertension. I wanted to single-handedly destroy the birthplace I hated, yet loved. In my stead, I asked that disaster strike it and that terror reign. Thus, the riots, when they happened, seemed to answer a prayer.

My rage was a lifetime deep.

That life began one year into President Harry S. Truman's first term (1945-1953). My tender years corresponded to General Dwight D. Eisenhower's term of office—1953 to 1961. My parents, migrants from mid- and southwest farming communities, voted Republican—Americans of African Descent who believed in 'Abe Lincoln's Party.' My mother worked as a domestic in the home of then-actor Ronald Reagan and wife Jane Wyman; quit, eventually becoming a seamstress. My father aspired to be a champion boxer. They hung on the periphery of an ambitious clique that gravitated around 'the talented tenth' (W.E.B. DuBois) of coloreds who had seemingly gained entré into the White world as artists, entertainers, and sports figures—singer Sarah Vaughan, painter Charles White, and Light Heavyweight champion Archie "The Old Mongoose" Moore (who actually hung around our house). Race aside, it wasn't what you knew, but who—went Pop's tried yet tired mantra on success.

My early days included parent-sponsored activities. They took me into the world of 4-H Clubs and lawn tennis. I experienced a wealth of cultural events, from concerts at Philharmonic Hall to the Shrine Auditorium, including those in which my father performed, singing Negro spiritual solos in the grand auditorium at the then-dazzling Golden State Insurance Company building as if he were Paul Robeson. Sunday mornings were usually spent at Price Chapel AME Church. We were poor—although I didn't know it—but not yet disenfranchised. A dollar, when one had it, stretched a long way. Like many of their peers, my parents scrimped to maintain a new automobile and a one-car garage home. This was done on my father's salary—once he gave up boxing—as an insurance agent, janitor, and house painter-cum-ad man. However, what started as an idyllic Negro youth in the Southern California of the '50s would quickly be aborted. I was about to enter the Los Angeles School System.

My parents had avoided explaining racism beyond strong warnings that others "out there" might try and make me feel inferior. I, too, was an American, they insisted, anyone's equal, regardless of race, color, or creed—words taken to heart despite a reality that would soon shake my confidence.

These were the days before Black was beautiful.

Outside home, I lived in a White world—Caucasians whose parents or grandparents had immigrated from Europe—Franco-Italian, Scotch-Irish, Danish-Swedish—and the like. When I started school, the black population was small, the student body in the schools I attended eighty-to-ninety percent White. Inside the classrooms, the children of immigrants received preferential treatment. The hands of teachers—females—were rough as they snatched my forearms to move me away from one spot or to another, one place to another, without any explanation except "You belong over here." In time, no explanation was required. The reason was obvious. I was soon a survivor of kindergarten and first grade bouts of being called 'nigger,' increasingly sensitized to the White authorities and low-toned males who preferred Negro girls with small bones, long pressed hair, and 'funny colored' eyes. Yet—the concept of racism remained amorphous, eluding my preadolescent expression.

This sad madness was compounded in 1952 by an influx of new schoolmates—the majority with lighter complexions—largely the offspring of migrants from Texas and the Old South, drawn west by jobs and a purportedly less racist social climate. Our Florence-Graham neighborhood housed several Rom (Gypsy) and Filipino families whose children also attended local public schools. The majority of migrant workers had once been Black, but that had quickly changed as Mexicans increasingly crossed the U.S. border to displace them. These new arrivals quickly adjoined Southern California's Negro subculture and its pecking order: if you light, you all right; if you black, get back, if you brown, stick around.

By second grade, I had heard of restricted housing and Blue Laws, but knew nothing about wards-of-the-United States or second-class citizenship, or the kind of hardships the children of these migrants had experienced. I had never heard of the paper bag test or soul food, much less Jim Crow. Along with folkways, regarded by our White teachers as superstitions, they brought with them an unparalleled wave of self-loathing, shame, and a remarkable fear of Whites I did not share. I would pay for my independent or 's'ditty' attitude during recess and after school, with my ego and knuckles. Among these new schoolmates, I would be branded ugly and undesirable.

I began to learn how to hate.

Likewise, I began to pray for freedom from hatred.

At school, as I walked the hallways, or dealt with whatever bull-corn awaited me on the school grounds, I prayed to be free of the ignorance and race hate that smothered my love of learning. I prayed that one day I would find a way to wear my hair in a manner others would accept—free of the stink of pine tar and growth pomades.

I recall—once—standing in a near-empty hallway, tardy as usual, facing a double flight of stairs, dreading the climb. I knew that the second I entered the classroom, I would face the ongoing ridicule garnered by my kinky grade of hair, bright eyes, toothy smile, and dark skin—not from the White students, the few Mexican, Asian-American, and Filipino students, or the teacher, but from my Black classmates.

When walking home alone after school, I would drift into crying jags that would end in dry retching and pugnacious resignation.

The only words I had ever heard that approached what I felt came ironically from the villainous lips of the Thuggee cult leader (Eduardo Ciannelli) in the film Gunga Din. My favorite part was the soliloquy in which he deplored the subjugation of his people by the British. To abort his capture as hostage, he jumps to his death. In my imaginary rewrite of the script, the Thuggees were victorious against the colonialists, my role a faithful follower who inspired her husband's sacrifice, or as the goddess Kali incarnate. I longed to be able to articulate what I saw as the psychosocial subjugation of my people—internalized racism—what I saw of it then, in hope that such an articulation might, in the sheer power of utterance, dispel it.

At the public library I researched the Thuggees, finding little. There was less on Mr. W.D. Fard and the Black Muslims—a cult that had once been compared to the Thuggees in a newspaper article. I had found the item among papers in my parents' portable mahogany liquor cabinet. From 1948, it concerned a sect that touted economic freedom for the Black man. My parents had never mentioned the Muslims and, when asked, could not satisfy my curiosity. They talked about Thurgood Marshall, Adam Clayton Powell, Philip A. Randolph, and the like. They read and discussed

James Baldwin, Richard Wright, and W.E.B. DuBois. But these leaders and heroes seldom came west, and their rhetoric and actions seemed to have little effect on my parents, as their lives became bleaker the blacker our neighborhood became—Whites fleeing the heart of the city, taking wealth and prosperity to the suburbs.

The hero I longed for did not seem to exist.

In August 1955, 14-year-old Chicagoan, Emmet Louis Till, was lynched in Money, Mississippi. Photographs of his corpse, in state, and the lines of hundreds of mourners, appeared in either *Ebony* or *Jet* magazine or both—they graced our living-room coffee table along with *Life* and *Look*. It was the first time I had ever heard of Whites lynching a Black child, although the mysterious or suspicious deaths of Negro juvenile males were frequent here at home and, not rarely, at the hands of Los Angeles police officers. Those violences seemed distant, therefore abstract. (I was two years away from learning about Nazi death camps and the fate of six million Jews, including children, when Alain Resnais's 1946 documentary Night and Fog was screened for Gompers Junior High seniors in 1960.) However, those photographs made Till's death brutally intimate. I stared at them for hours. His murder seemed harbinger of the social change I longed for at the beginning of each school day.

But by 1958, the only changes in Los Angeles seemed to be the arrival of the Brooklyn Dodgers, the destruction of Chavez Ravine's neighborhoods—LA's first Jewish settlement turned Mexican-American, and a remarkable surge in White flight. As the complexions of students in my classrooms darkened, I found myself in a constant state of inexpressible rage, ping-ponging between thoughts of mass homicide or suicide. My childhood diaries are full rant. ("July 20th 1961—Can I help it if my hair is short? Damn everyone who makes cracks at it…I feel like hell.") I hated school. My stomach flip-flopped continually on my fifteen-minute walks from home to campus. My hatred had become physical. I did not know how to discuss this anguish with my parents, or anyone. I became moody and brooded about the house, to their consternation. My grades dropped and I began to get into trouble. A rage was blossoming within me fertilized by the insistent logic that any concept of self-pride must include skin tone and everything that went with it.

As much as I hated school, I loved the poetry I had been introduced to by a first grade teacher. Surely poems, even if poets didn't make googobs of money, were magically transformative—as was all art. I became the child who always excelled when writing something original, a poem for father's day or a story for Christmas. Somehow, I thought, if I could master my inarticulation, I could master my rage, and not only change myself through my writings, but transform the hateful world I knew into a place I could love. More importantly—a place that would love me back.

Then—in 1959, we watched a TV documentary titled The Hate that Hate Produced. My parents were shocked yet intrigued, although agreeing with the documentary's point of view. I was thrilled and electrified by the appearance of 'fine looking' (Mother's description) Malcolm X—who openly addressed the subjugation of Negro people with as great a fire as Mr. Ciannelli in his role as Thuggee kingpin. But Malcolm X was a real man. My hero did exist!

Malcolm X visited Los Angeles in 1961 (the year J.F.K. was inaugurated), during a period when gang activity was so intense, the transit system was refusing to allow Negro students on public buses without passes guaranteeing they were not gang members. One morning, as I rushed to school, I forgot my pass. The bus driver actually closed the door on my ankle, trapping my foot inside. He did not drive away, but, after a few hops, released it. I walked the hour to Gompers, missing homeroom and first period. I was not in a gang but was paying for the stigma. I belonged, as I would say two decades later, to that larger 'gang', the Black race.

As if coinciding with Malcolm's visit, rumors of an underground surge of Black pride began circulating through South Central. Freedom was increasingly whispered about on campus at John C. Fremont High, during recess, lunch, and after school at the clubs that met for extracurricular activities. It was spoken of in soft tones by adults in the neighborhood. It was confirmed by White teachers who stormed the school district by the hundreds with requests to transfer out of inner city schools where the student body had become predominately Afro-American. We knew the White teachers who feared us. They had taught us well how to hate them.

On November 23, 1963, John Fitzgerald Kennedy was assassinated, and the promise of the "Affluent '60s" began to evaporate.

By 1964, the civil rights movement was dominating headline news. But LA's Negro bourgeois elite sniggered at civil rights activists like Martin Luther King in private quarters and closed meetings. My parents sided with these conservative Negroes who did not want the associated violence in their communities, no matter how nonviolent they were supposed to be—those boycotts, hunger strikes, sit-ins, and marches. While the civil rights movement never reached Southern California, a militant political activism was emerging on campuses and in enclaves. In a May 1963 issue of Muhammad Speaks, an article appeared in which Malcolm X accused LA's Mayor Yorty of running a "Ku Klux Klan police force." It jolted the city. "Friends of" networks were organizing underground meetings and fundraisers. That year future mayor Thomas (Tom) Bradley would become the first Black to be elected to the city council. My worried parents broadcast their hopes and opinions loudly around the dinner table—for my benefit.

43

I listened quietly.

There was a strange new construction going on in the inner city. Our stately schools, built before WWII, were beginning to resemble prisons. Certain sections were sealed off, the green quads and court-yards placed off limits or paved over. Bungalows appeared as class sizes grew, decreasing area available for playground activities. Calculus, Greek, Latin, and Journalism were among the classes that disappeared from the curriculum. In the November 1964 election, a local Fair Housing Act proposition was defeated by White voters—which managed to anger my parents, who still begrudged the restricted housing that had crippled their chances for economic stability in the early years of their marriage.

At home, my parents began to fail economically as the price of material things out-climbed their combined incomes. My father could no longer find fruitful employment, abandoned the Republican Party and became a Democrat. My mother's paycheck as a seamstress was steadily eroded by bosses bringing in cheaper labor from Mexico. I was exiting puberty, and it was more than obvious that they could not send me to college. My hatred for Los Angeles increased exponentially.

Within six months, between June and November of 1964, I grad-uated from high school, started college, turned eighteen, left home, married, dropped out of college, threw away my hot-iron pressing comb and curler to go au naturel, and joined LA's political underground. Nine months later, I would give birth to my first child. Days later, in August 1965 (the violence raging three days before being reported in local newspapers), Watts erupted in flames.

Black had become beautiful.

I lived in a Black world.

From the ashes in Watts sprang a series of arts and educational organizations that opened their doors to encourage Black writers and artists. I joined a creative arts workshop, writing plays and poems. Whenever I ran into old classmates, they were usually embarrassed. Malcolm X was assassinated on February 21, 1965. Martin Luther King was stilled on April 4, 1968. In August of 1968, James Brown screamed "Say it loud, I'm Black and I'm proud" over the airwaves. My first husband and I were remarried as orthodox Muslims, but it would not save our marriage. The civil rights movement was declared over by 1969. Except for programs at the Watts Towers and Inner City Cultural Center, similar programs in Watts, funded during President Lyndon Johnson's (1963-69) War on Poverty, would vanish by 1975—two years before the debut of my first poetry chapbook. My exorcism of old hatreds by writing had begun, but the transformation was elusive. A second marriage and a new child were on my horizon.

By the end of the '70s, I had again divorced to become a single working mother, dropping in-and-out of college while working full time. Whatever job sustained me—magazine editor, waitress, proofreader—at whatever interval, I groped to fulfill the promise made to that younger self. I stayed the difficult course—as the years fled, no matter the diversion or distraction, through broken relationships and ceaseless crises that attend the working-class poor. I became an accomplished writer, but the world I had known was disappearing under the relentless pressures of economic disparity—as the unresolved issues of redlining, police brutality, poverty, and drugs continued to fester, and new, more voracious, youth gangs sprang from the asphalt.

Unable to get steady work as a scriptwriter, I entered the pink-collar working class, moonlighting as a bartender. Between 1979 and 1989, I had skipped vacations, sacrificed sleep and any available spare time to produce seven collections of stories and poems with Black Sparrow, a literary press. But prestige is hard to eat. The boss who refused to give my mother a raise to feed her family had become President Reagan (1981-1989). Mother had voted for him, despite her history. Towards the end of that horrific decade, during which my father's health declined, she would receive a rude cut in her social security check and regret her ballot. I began teaching occasionally, traveling and lecturing with my poetry. But that was not enough.

In 1991, following the death of my father, I took a major risk and quit my 'slave' as medical secretary, encouraged by my third husband of ten years. The pull of my gift could no longer be denied. I had to write—regardless. I was in my mid-forties. Other than temporary layoffs, it was the first time since 1972 that I had been without a regular paycheck. Ahead, lay disaster—spun from the ever-complex machinations of race. Mother would soon remarry only to become a widow for the second time. With the help of a friend, I scored a new script agent and began crawling Hollywood's pitch dens. Renewed pursuits as scriptwriter and journalist, promising at first, did not work out. Then, on April 29, 1992, as I left a late morning meeting at the Department of Cultural Affairs, the verdict by the Simi Valley jury in the Rodney King beating case was announced. Afternoon into evening, I drove the city from downtown to Hollywood, through the Crenshaw district, then Westwood. By the time I arrived home the city was again in flames, after twenty-seven years—for virtually the same reasons.

As I watched the coverage, I was struck by newscasters who repeatedly referred to rioters as 'thugs.' They didn't grasp the meaning of the word. I recalled Mr. Ciannelli's performance and wished. But like the headless hens I had once watched flop around the farmyard, after my grandmother had wrung their necks, the various outcroppings of violence spent themselves and collapsed, leaving residues of fear and more hate. As factions struggled through curfew toward recovery, it was apparent that the issues of South Central Los Angeles, the same issues that had affected my parents in the postwar Los Angeles of the late '40s and '50s, and which circumscribed my lifetime, would largely go unaddressed.

Yet another decade has passed. The new century my father did not live to see has begun.

As I write, the 35th anniversary of the Watts Riots has just passed and the 10th anniversary of the South Central LA Riots approaches. As I prepared this essay, I spent a week gathering various clips from my extensive collection from which to extrapolate and draw statistics. (I began keeping them in 1959, the first for a current events report for History class on Fidel Castro's overthrow of the Batista Regime.) I think of Attica (1971), Philadelphia's Operation MOVE (1985), and the O.J. Simpson Trial (1996). But the clips I favored were those documenting the 27-year-terror of racism against African Americans in California, emphasis on LA. They detail a multileveled domestic assault—economic, educational, financial, psycho-social—in law enforcement and entertainment, everything from the Bakke case to The Peoples Temple and Jonestown to an item on Black women as the favored targets of airport security searches. As I scanned them, I was again reminded of how much a statistic I had become. I put them aside to consider how this particular statistic should bring itself to life—personally.

Then, something unexpected and incredibly tremendous happened. On Tuesday morning, September 11th, America sustained an assault on the Pentagon and the catastrophic destruction of the nation's financial heart, New York City's World Trade Center. Nineteen men—thugs—presumably of Arab or Afghani descent, martyred themselves, commandeering four jet passenger liners. Three of those transports-turned-bombs struck their targets. They extinguished the lives of an estimated six-thousand innocent people on American soil, roughly 1/1000th of the number of lives lost in the Nazi concentration camps. I thought about the 64,000 at Nagasaki and the 135,000 at Hiroshima. I thought about learning that rocks bleed. I thought about my draft-age son.

WWIII has been declared. The transformation has begun.

Like the majority of citizens, I watched—and still watch—the daily news reports, seeking signs of the tumult ahead. What role can I play, other than lighting candles, making donations, writing letters to friends? What does a poet do when poetry is the most under-appreciated art in a nation—even considered subversive—where the images manufactured in Hollywood (largely negative images of Blacks) are "it's second largest export," to quote Chicago Tribune journalist Clarence Page. But....

Being who I am, I can't not make note of the ironies—of the arrogance governing our nation's rhetoric, its military and intelligence agencies, and the misology that governs the mindset of our predominately Caucasian leadership of immigrant descent. In an email to a kindred spirit who resides in Washington, D.C., I posed rhetorically: "Did ageism, homophobia, racism, and sexism die in the Attack on America?"

He did not answer and I did not pursue the issue.

After four straight days of round-the-clock viewing, I decided I had to get out of the house and drive out to the cemetery. I had not visited my father's grave in over a year. I did as usual, took grass clippers, a rag, and bottled water, got down on my knees and tidied up, asking, as I usually do, the unanswerable.

It was Saturday noon, the sky was overcast, and the grounds deserted. When I finished, I walked the hill overlooking west Los Angeles—Century City Plaza and beyond. This, I thought, is the city my father loved, in which he died unfulfilled, if well into his seventies. The plaque that marks his spot in the underworld was paid for by my book royalties. Mother has never visited the site.

It was over before I knew it was happening. That is what I remember most about the days of rage in the city of my birth.

I wish I could say I had been here, that I had experienced the numbing shock of the verdict, that I had felt the sting of smoke in my eyes, or that I could show calluses on my hands, rubbed raw with the clean-up of so much that was shattered in those few days.

But instead, I spent April 29 and the days that followed in Marrakech, Morocco. I was a college student traveling the world, oblivious to what was unfolding 6,000 miles away.

The news came by telephone on May 2, after I had spent three days out of touch, exploring Marrakech's medina and reveling in a city that was such an amalgam of races and languages and cultures that it almost—but not quite—felt like home. I was a foreigner there, and compelled by an aching sense of homesickness, I gathered all of the five- and 10-dirham coins I had. Fifty of them—about $6—bought me a call to America from a public telephone. On my third try, the call went through, crackling just a bit, as it rang. My mother answered.

"We're all OK, after the riots," she said to me as soon as she heard my voice, assuming that the premise of my call was more than just simple homesickness or a need to connect with family.

"The riots?" I asked quizzically, unable to imagine what she could mean.

"Oh honey," I heard her sigh. "You'd better get a paper."

The two-minute conversation ended with a dull clicking sound on the line. I rushed to a newsstand across the street, where all that remained was a single copy of *USA Today*, its cover picture a menacing fire over a city that looked strangely familiar. The headline was stark and syncopated: "City Under Siege, Curfew Ordered, Guard Moves In." I felt cold. There was no global CNN for me to turn to then, no hour-by-hour recap of events as they unfolded. And so I surrendered quickly to the realization that these bits and pieces of information would be all that I would know. "24 dead, 18 by gunfire," the paper cried. "$100 million in damages." Life in Marrakech was marching on around me as I sank into a chair to take in the news. There would be no empathetic outpouring of emotion there for the people in Los Angeles, no easy way to keep vigil or share songs of unity and hope.

I was alone.

In later days, it would occur to me that I had seen a hint of what was to come, or some inkling of what had happened, in a newspaper head-line that I had carelessly read off someone else's paper in a café the day before. Violence à Los Angeles it read in French, violence in the city I loved. I had casually dismissed it then as an excoriation of the sins of the celluloid city by the French-language press.

Perhaps that says something about my—and our—pre-riot mentality, that I could so casually dismiss the violence, the rage, as commonplace. But perhaps it means that nothing in my twenty years, or even after, prepared me to understand what had occurred. My daily letters home after the phone call never discussed the riots, never asked probing questions, or sought explanations for how everything could have happened so quickly.

The only time I mentioned the events at all was almost two weeks later, when I wrote saying that French friends "wanted to talk about racism and Los Angeles, a subject which I find hard enough to explain in English."

"I can't give a good analysis," I continued, "of a situation that seems so far away, especially since my growing up years were so shattered from urban blight."

But even after I flew home, sixteen days after the riots had begun, I could do no better. I still felt tongue-tied, as if I had no right to offer an opinion. I saw the boarded-up windows, the charred hulls of people's worlds. But I never recaptured the immediacy of their rage or the urgency of the crisis.

Once in a while, I will hear tales: of a friend who stood watch on a roof top in West LA and saw the night sky lit up as if it were dawn; of the Los Angeles Times editor who fended off would-be rioters with a pair of scissors, the only weapon in his arsenal. These stories have become a sort of Los Angeles mythology for me, tentative explanations of what happened in those few short days.

And so I returned to this city on the edge—a city that as long as I live here, I will never again fully understand.

52

THE SMELL OF RAGE

Kitty Felde

For me, the riots began in a parking lot in Simi Valley. I was a public radio reporter, covering the criminal trial of the four Los Angeles police officers accused of beating Rodney King. Every day, for nine long months, I made the forty-five minute drive out the 118 freeway to Simi Valley—a sleepy little town surrounded by grassy foothills where Hollywood used to make westerns—until suburbia crept in. Now instead of cowboys, the city was home to vast numbers of LA police officers.

The jury had been out for days and days. Bored journalists had put up their dollars for a pool to guess the exact time the jury would return a verdict. My dollar was on lunchtime, April 29th. A court watcher in the parking lot told me he'd had a dream the night before that the verdict would come down today, just after noon. I won the pool—190 dollars. As the day unfolded, it turned out to be the most inappropriate wager I ever made in my life.

As the jury filed into the courtroom, radio journalists like me were huddled next to our tape recorders in the press room next door. Listening. This was my first "real" trial—instead of dropping in for opening statements and closing arguments, I'd been given the freedom to attend every day of court, listening to every bit of testimony. Green as I was, I expected convictions. I reasoned that the jury had seen the infamous videotape over and over and over again. If prosecutors couldn't convict with evidence like that, I thought, they had no business in court.

But when the verdicts were read, I felt like I'd been socked in the stomach. Not guilty. Not guilty. Not guilty. Not guilty. And I thought: if I felt this betrayed and angry, how would the rest of the city feel? And how would people react? I already knew the answer.

I grew up in Compton, just a couple of miles south of Watts. I remembered my eleventh birthday in 1965 when Watts exploded into six days of looting and burning and rioting. The smell of smoke hung in the air for weeks.

I also remember watching the "white flight" in action—hungry realtors licking their chops as they stuck fliers under the door of nervous white folks, warning them that their property values would plummet to nothing unless they sold out now. My parents refused to budge. They believed in Dr. King's vision of a country where kids of all colors could dream together. Instead of 4th of July picnics, I was dragged to civil rights marches and unity breakfasts. When my family finally moved away in 1974 after the divorce, we may have been the last white family in Compton.

As I sat at my desk in Simi Valley, trying to compose a story, my stomach in knots, I remembered that smell of smoke from my 11th birthday. And after the lawyers' press conference, I happened to look out the second floor window. I saw it start, right there in the parking lot. Angry people surrounded the defense attorneys' cars, shouting, pounding on the windows. People started throwing punches at each other. It was unreal, like a scene from a movie. I called my news director to tell him what I was seeing. And if people were angry forty-five minutes away from everything, imagine how much more intense that anger would be in the heart of the city. And it was.

There were cell phones in 1992—sort of. They were anything but pocket size and attached to bulky batteries that weighed as much as a frozen turkey and our station had just one. The phone was handed over to my colleague Frank Stoltze who spent most of the next week out on the front lines. I protested loudly when I was sent to press conference after press conference, but the truth is that I was glad Frank was being sent into the battle zone. I had no taste for the front lines. Especially after I heard stories of colleagues whose vans were broken into and reporters who were beaten. I was no war reporter and I knew it.

Instead, I was sent with my tape recorder to a fancy restaurant high atop the Transamerica Tower where LA Mayor Tom Bradley and Cardinal Roger Mahoney appealed for calm. But the city's top leaders began losing their audience as one by one, reporters turned their attention away from the podium and out the window. There below us was the city of Los Angeles, where you could see the flames and smoke from dozens and dozens of fires.

As the days of rioting went on, the fires and the looting spread to many neighborhoods and shopping districts—including the Fedco store where I'd left my grandfather's watch. I'd given it to my husband as a wedding gift just four months earlier. But the watch wasn't keeping good time, so I took it to Fedco for repairs. As I watched the helicopter pictures of looters running out the doors, carrying armloads of Fedco merchandise, I mentally wrote off the watch. (Months later Fedco reopened and the Middle Eastern watchmaker told a too familiar immigrant's tale: He had lost everything in the riots—dozens of Rolex watches, his watch repair equipment, none of it covered by insurance. But an accident of fate saved my grandfather's watch. The watchmaker had taken it home where he thought he had an old part that might fit. I nearly cried when he put the pocket watch in my hands, keeping perfect time.)

For my colleague Frank Stoltze, the three days of rioting meant three days of nonstop reporting. But by the weekend, when it was deemed safe to travel without a cell phone, it was my turn to walk the streets to look for stories. That first weekend, small bands of people wandered from neighborhood to neighborhood, this time carrying brooms and shovels. I watched as folks of every ethnic persuasion approached the shell-shocked shopkeepers and asked if they could help clean up. I saw others walking the streets with voter registration forms. It was hard to imagine that there was something as simple as a city election just weeks away. Especially when there were National Guard tanks still parked down the street.

For me, the riots came to an end weeks after the fires were out and the tanks had gone home. City officials were tallying up the damage and sociologists were starting to ask "why?" Federal prosecutors were putting together a civil rights case against the four Los Angeles police officers accused of beating Rodney King. And I made a very bad driving decision. I was trying to make a left turn onto a busy street and I just didn't see the blue Toyota. We both swerved. She honked, I swore my usual litany of obscenities at myself for doing something lame brained. We both pulled over to the curb, shaking. "What did you say?" the driver screamed at me. She was out of the car in a moment, followed by two large men and another woman. "What did you say?"

I repeated my string of obscenities, in a small voice, verbatim. "Oh," she said, "I thought you'd called me 'nigger.'"

"God, no," I told her.

"Huh. All right then," she said, and drove off with her friends. I sat there shaking.

This is how it was in Los Angeles for a long, long time. The city cleaned up the burned buildings. And put up fencing around what were now vacant lots. Businesses reopened. Or they didn't. Corporations pledged to make jobs available in poor neighborhoods. Some didn't. But the city itself was on edge. Angry. Hurt. Scared. Walking on eggshells.

It wasn't until the Northridge earthquake two years later that the anger finally began to fade. Suddenly we weren't "them" and "us." We were all shaken up and frightened. We were all cowed by the quake. Some lost everything, some lost a few jars of pickle relish. But for those of us who survived, we had a stake in the survival and well-being of each other. We had become a community again.

But for how long? What would it take for another meltdown?

Our challenge began again on September 11th, 2001. When planes crashed into the World Trade Center Towers and the Pentagon, official fingers were quickly pointed at terrorist cells from the Middle East. There were fears that the community of southern California would take out its anger on the local Muslim and Middle Eastern community.

But it seems we have learned something since 1991. Those shaky bridges built to connect communities after the unrest were still open.

Christian and Jewish communities reached out to their Muslim colleagues for interfaith services and teach-ins. When right-wing talk shows called for internment camps for Arab-Americans, Japanese-Americans organized public forums to say, "no, never again." And while there were isolated incidents of violence and hate crimes around Southern California, there were also countless examples of individuals who wanted to "hug a Muslim": a man who volunteered to escort Afghan grandmothers to the grocery store, the woman who donned a head scarf in solidarity, bouquets of flowers dropped off at mosques.

Los Angeles is indeed the grand experiment in diversity. If we can't find a way to make it work here, what hope is there for the rest of the world?

58

DREAMINGS OF
THE DEAD

Ramón García   59

The city air still smelled of smoke. Helicopters circled the sky, dipping closer to ground at night, streaking the dark above the city with searchlights. It was a week since the '92 riots had started and the fires were finally out. At Arena Disco nothing had changed. The smoke machines spewed icy clouds from the ground up; they rose, ghostly, to disperse and evaporate in the masses of bodies. Strobe lights convulsed extremities of light and dark, flickering maniacally to the speeded tempo of the music. Outside, the police, ambulance, and fire department sirens screamed into the night. Albert ordered another round of tequila shots. Diane brought her tequila shot glass up to eye level and we clicked glasses. We were celebrating Diane's 25th birthday.

A raised catwalk cut the stadium-size dance floor in half—drag queens were strutting down it, sashaying haughtily to the rhythm of haute couture music. It was a fashion show. Diane downed a shot, looking at the Arena scene in disgusted disbelief. "Goddamn, fuckin' drag-queens," she shouted over the scratchy techno music rattling the walls and the dance floor. "The fires are barely out. Ash is still falling from the sky. The world could be burning down in flames, but those horse-faced bitches would still be worried about their wigs, their make-up, and their fashion and their bullshit! This city is fucked up…"

I didn't say anything. I didn't want to think about it. I wanted to be taken in by the spectacle, the assault of fake smoke, music, disco balls that threw swirling glitter patches of illuminated squares like a confetti of stars upon the crowds.

I asked the bartender for another round.

Ash had been falling from the sky that day. You could see the ashen film on the hoods of cars in the Target parking lot. The National Army tanks had withdrawn from the streets the day before and that night would be the first without curfew. On Robertson Boulevard the blackened shards of burnt down Korean grocery stores were the skeletal reminders that something terrible had happened. I looked up at the cloudless sky, curtained by the leaden layers of the riot's smog. I never saw the sky like that again, like a rusty shadow hanging over the city, portending nothing.

I was turning thirty that year and the new batch of boys on the dance floor were starting to look younger and younger. Standing naked in front of the full-length mirror I sucked in my belly. My waif days were over and I was too lazy to do anything about it. I was still not adapted to LA. I didn't belong to any gym. And so I wasn't looking like the kin of the Arena boys anymore, but like a member of a closely related, but lesser species. There is an unofficial expiration date on gay nightlife, and it's mercilessly definitive. It's advisable to retire from Arena at thirty because the dance floor is like the boxing ring, it's only for the young and cute who are willing to get hurt for the glory. You can't compete with the freshness of the new ones streaming in every week. Your looks no longer make you a winner, no matter how striking you were when you started out on the dance floor at nineteen. It's best to call it a dignified quits.

At twenty-two you instinctively sense that despite all that you logically know about mortality, time will not erode the omnipower of youth. You aspire to live in the magical aura of an Interview magazine fashion ad, sporting the style that contains the dream of love and wealth in a pose. The drinking and the drugs fuel those dreams. On the Arena dance floor everything was magically canceled: poverty, the uncertain future, problems at home, the difficulties of work, and surviving. We believed those moments of strobe-lighted rapture were a sort of salvation, that the ecstasy worked up in the frenzy of the music was all that we needed, all that life could possibly offer. But we had doubts—that we never spoke of, that we did not know how to articulate and misunderstood, that we feared would infringe on the restless search for something that would take us out of ourselves.

"Do you think we'll be friends ten, twenty years from now?" Diane said with seriousness, shading her stoned, blood-shot eyes, winged in glittery purple. The bartender rudely slammed two shot glasses of tequila in front of us. He was of that breed of gay men who do not like fag hags and Diane screamed fag hag—overweight, attitude, funky thrift shop retro clothes. "That faggot prick," she said glancing at the bartender as he moved away. "Sometimes I think there's some kind of conspiracy against being deep around here, having a normal conversation like normal human beings! I was being serious here." She tossed the shot glass of tequila into her mouth after licking salt off her hand. She bit into a quarter slice of lime, grimacing with its bitterness. "I was asking you question," Diane awkwardly continued. "Do you think we'll be friends forever, even when we are old and shriveled up and senile?"

"Yeah, I guess," I said. I was impressed with Diane's ambition to be "deep" at Arena. "We've been friends for a while—"

"Five years, that's a long time around here." There was a defensive distaste on her face as she looked at the boys on the dance floor, in front of us. "A lot of these people are very superficial," she lamented. "Everything is disposable to them. Friendship, sex, identity. One day they are one thing and the next they are something else. It's kind of psycho, but everyone thinks that's normal. Sometimes I think even their own lives are disposable. They're like a mutant species, the disposable people."

I downed my shot glass. The cheap tequila felt bitter as it went down my throat, it settled on my stomach like a lump of burning heat. It gave me the courage to be frank and sentimental. I said, "I'm glad we're not like that Diane."

"Yeah, I'm glad too." Her eyes became teary. She laughed, holding on to her composure. "Let's go dance," she said, pepping herself up. She looked for Albert on the dance floor until she spotted him. "That's enough bullshit for tonight, you silly *joto*." She smiled, her embarrassment fading. We joined Albert and danced until the 4:00 a.m. closing time.

I realized that I was half in love with Santos. Not with a love made of sexual passion or physical attraction, but a more perverse and platonic affection, the way we love an abusive helplessness in others, or a comforting illness. I saw myself in him, saw what I wanted to see of myself in him. But I never suspected we were living in a minor holocaust, the dark night of our common lives.

Arena belongs to another life. I live in Fresno now. A world away from Los Angeles. A life apart from the person I was there. I am going to tell you about my time in Los Angeles, because I have chewed over it the last four years and I am ready to put it to rest. I have a superstitious belief that if I write it all down I can finally bury the hatchet that I have swung at my own shadow, that I confused for Santos, Rudy, and Jesse. I have used up all my resentment of them, and discovered in its place my own particular exile and sense of irretrievable loss. I spent a little more than a year there. Not all that long.

I made friends and lost them. I can look back and understand how we all played a part in destroying the life we had built together. I can revisit the characters that peopled my life in LA and I can somehow get a grasp on who they were and why I was mistaken in the end. It's much harder for me to account for who I was back then, what I was doing, but there it is.

In my closet I have kept a slice of the LA life: a portfolio filled with Santos' photos that was given to me by his sister, Mari. The last time I saw her, she said, "He would have liked you to have these." I told her to keep them, that perhaps it was a better thing for her to keep them. But she wouldn't listen. I didn't want them then and I'm not sure I want them now, but I couldn't destroy them, Santos' images, Santos' art, Santos' life, our life. I began to sort through it. All those nights in LA returned as I flipped through those photographs, memories culled from some subterranean life belonging to Santos, containing both us and the human wreckage of the city. All the photographs were taken at night (in a state of intoxication of course), as if no images of the marginal life could be summoned out of the moderate daytime.

Sorting through the stack of photographs, so many LA scenes pass through my fingers: there is Rudy, in drag, wearing a straight black wig with a Corona bottle in his hand at that first party early in the year; there is Jesse smiling, cocktail in hand, at Santos' New Year's Eve party, and I am blurred in the background; there is a Mexican drag queen grabbing her crotch with both hands as she leans against the bathroom wall next to a Pissoir in the Plaza men's bathroom; there is a sexily-dressed midget wearing pornographic high heel shoes, sitting on top of the stove in Santos' kitchen, at one of his dinner parties that remains dimly in my mind. Then there were the photographs of bleeding saints and wounded Mexican Christs taken in Mexican churches, the countless frozen gestures of singers and drag queens in Mexico City, the drug addicts in grimy rooms in downtown LA, and their Mexican and Cuban versions in Mexico City and Cuba. All those sordidly splendorous images that ended up destroyed or dispersed by the tides of carelessness and neglect, the legacy of a life lived irregularly, with frenzied purposelessness. I sensed Santos' presence in those images, like the secret witness of our damage, still watching over us, recording it through the wonder of his own disintegration.

64

WAITING FOR THE RAINBOW SIGN

Lynell George

By midnight, no one phoning long distance bothers with hello. Instead, they just ask, "Is it as crazy as it looks?"

I want to say, "It started long before all this..." Long before this afternoon's bewildering decision left me less astonished than strangely numb. Long before George Holliday ran tape capturing Rodney G. King's struggle and submission. Long before Latasha Harlins, Eulia Love, and Marquette Frye became cautionary symbols. Long before Watts shouted its existence into the sky in '65, sending up searchlights in the form of flames.

They want me to make sense of footage I'm mesmerized by, of the faces that register riot gear. Familiar landscape altered by skewed aerial views and flame. I try to put into simple words what I've seen and heard in the last few hours of this day.

Until I can see it up close, with my own eyes, I'm relying on sound—and video—bites as if they were air: first the radio reports of an "intentional" accident at Florence and Normandie; 100 to 150 people sprinting through intersections at rush hour; the new bloody chaos at Normandie and 70th. Mayor Tom Bradley, whose face doesn't seem able to accommodate any more fatigue, standing solemn at the pulpit at First African Methodist Episcopal Church, tries not to flinch when pelted with boos. Local ministers use their melodious baritones frantically to implement "Operation Cool Head." Too late. By sundown rocks and bottles sail toward the windshields of passing cars, through store windows, at nothing in particular. Random debris jams the city works.

I'm in a press of traffic motoring east on Washington. It thins dramatically when I swing south on La Brea to Adams. My wide stretch of boulevard, gateway to black LA's Sugar Hill of the '40s. Old churches, big trees, even bigger houses. A place that seldom before surfaced for the world as representative of Black LA. But no doubt the world will see it now. At Crenshaw, I see what has been sketchily described on the radio for the last couple hours: figures rendered to silhouettes, occupying the street, advancing randomly. Shouting, laughing, they drift on foot into traffic, into the beams of headlights, as if they are truly invincible.

My tires eat glass, trundle over big, splintered husks of plywood, of brick, and clods of dirt. On my left I see a waterfall of glass. I don't hear the sound of it breaking: this scene has no soundtrack, no narrative line to hold on to. Out the other window I watch six pairs of hands pry apart white iron security gates. Here I see an ironic twist on the multiethnic coalition that local community leaders have been talking about for years, but not successfully implementing: black and Latino teenagers coming together to lift a sofa out of a furniture store's showcase window, onto shoulders, then down the sidewalk.

As a reflex, I'm already speedily taking notes, as if the act of writing down what I see and what I hear will bring about some sense of order. Clarity. But my handwriting turns out looking like angry, spiky hieroglyphics. Automatic writing. Subjects without predicates. Issues without resolution.

I don't head toward First AME for answers. I know that right now there are none to be had. Maybe the warmth of others equally confused, or moving toward sadness or rage will thaw my numbness. When the decision was passed down, I wasn't sure how to process the information; I didn't know how to respond to Powell's smile, to interpret Daryl Gates' barely suppressed grin; to understand my own emptiness.

Closer to the church, spectators have left cars all over, along red painted curbsides, in driveways, in loading zones, abandoned at the center of the road. Those of us circling for parking places are told to move on. Since the streets have quickly heated up, the 24-hour vigil has been canceled. Praying in public tonight is too dangerous. I smell alcohol in the air, strong, oozing out of broken glass that has hit the pavement. Then come the stones. Random. They thud against the thin metal of my car. Random, I slowly understand, we're in the heat of chaos.

I wind back to Adams. At the corner of Western, where looms the Golden State Mutual Life insurance company (an early monument to African-American business ingenuity and tenacity in Los Angeles), two men set fire to a wooden bus bench. The first flames are weak. They egg it on with words first, look around for something to stoke it—paper, wood, maybe a piece of their own clothing. I watch transfixed for too long as the fire leaps, changes in color. I remain because I know that tomorrow I will not recognize this corner. I want to preserve what I see now. Over radio static, I hear City Councilman Mark Ridley-Thomas on the radio composing his thoughts carefully: "...we haven't recovered from Watt's yet..." I conjure a picture of familiar city driving, down Martin Luther King, Arlington, Jefferson, other wide central-city "business" corridors, looking at row upon row of run-down nothing. Dilapidated façades with decaying or neglected interiors. Never been rebuilt, no plans to even begin. My foot trembles as I lift it from the brake, to place it on the accelerator, heading east, heading home. It tremors, I realize, not with fear but with rage, and I'm relieved that I finally feel something. Problem is, as always, I don't know what to do with it, or who will hear.

"Go home, stay home. Lock your doors." -KFWB 980 AM, Thursday, April 30

I've already seen the look.

Driving through the Silver Lake hills to avoid Sunset Boulevard's panicked snarl, I climb along the incline. People are out jogging and walking their dogs, even though fires have moved closer, are no longer a distant TV hell. The higher I climb, the more I see residents take note of my car's make and color; they mentally record the license number, but most importantly, my unfamiliar deep-brown face, any distinguishing marks. They look at me as if they will at any moment join together to form a human barricade if I make a wrong or abrupt move. Later, across town, a blond man in the next lane looks over LA pickup casual, then quickly lifts his smoked-glass window.

The same video feeds that have inspired their terror have fueled my own curiosity, augmented my pain. For hours I've been trans-fixed, watching childhood landmarks swallowed up in the surpris-ingly liquid aspects of billowing smoke and flames—stores, streets, memories, futures. I'm watching my old neighborhood blister, turn to embers, rendered entirely foreign. I hear fear in the voices of my relatives and friends who've been trying to track the course of the flames, guess the trajectory of anger.

"If you've got your ass out here you might get shot," one seen-it-all onlooker tells me. We're standing near the corner of Walton and Jefferson looking at the remains of a corner Mom & Pop still smol-dering, a single red flicker looking like some eerie twist on an eternal flame. "Brothers getting busy," he backs it up recounting the stagger-ing list of firearms he's seen the past week, from shotguns to .357 Magnums to Uzis. "They shut everything down early last night. I went down on Arlington, everybody started hitting the pawnshops. It was kids, old women, not just like criminals, like they've been saying on TV. It's like a free-for-all. Get it while you can. Let's roll and see what's poppin', " says my newly self-appointed guide.

"The message was there, but the method was wrong," offers one of the playground prophets chillin' at Denker Recreation Center. "We've inconvenienced ourselves now," he says, looking into the sul-fur-tinted sky. Fires loom around us, sirens scream, puddles of water left by pump trucks look more like polluted lakes. "Folks are gonna start getting real hungry down here. RTD shut down, people don't have cars."

"It's sad to me 'cause I grew up here and now they're burning it down," says the office manager from a Century City law firm. He has his hair cut into a neat, close fade and is still wearing his pink shirt and paisley tie with a square knot; a pager is clipped to his belt. "I had to drive over and check on my relatives," he explains. "I don't agree with the looting but I understand the frustration."

"I'll put it in two words," a woman strolling by, looking at my notebook tells me, "FUCKED UP." She wants to make sure that I've underlined the words, that they stand out somehow from all the rest on the page. "Two words, 'fucked up.' We hurt our folks the most. We deal with that. People scared to open up their shops today. Scared to walk out on the street."

As the burned-out buildings multiply, look more disfigured, more abstract as they collapse upon themselves, the stories become more tragic. Like the little boy who's decided not to leave the cement back yard behind his house because "I don't want to get caught by no police. I don't want to have to go through that." There is Francis, bewildered, who stands in front of the Church of God of Prophecy on Western, watching his electronics business smolder. "What...do...I...feel?" he asks the dead space before him. "What do I feel now? Upset. Angry. We as black people have been told that we could achieve anything if we put our mind to it. Now, because of a couple of days, it's going to take twenty or thirty years before we can achieve anything again. People here complain about South Africa. It is no better here."

69

"The arrogance of Gates, I believe, caused the whole thing," a security guard tells me as we watch a van pull up full of teens, loading up bottles of soda and alcohol. One offers me a cool drink. I decline with a shake of the head. "They've created a monster," the security guard continues, "Now they have to feed him."

"It's now 7:30 p.m. If you're on the street now you're breaking the law." -KFWB 980 AM, Friday, May 1

I've seen a number of objects lifted up and out of open windows of automobiles in motion. Brandished with a purpose. Each day it's been a different symbol. Wednesday it was a baseball bat shaken belligerently to the down-deep beats of DJ Quick as a long yellow Cadillac took St. Andrews Place at an estimated eighty mph. Thursday it was a clenched fist raised to all passers-by on the Crenshaw strip. On Friday, snaking down Stocker, it was a well-worn broom.

Crenshaw Boulevard traffic is sluggish since all the signals are out for blocks after exiting the freeway. No one has the time to direct traffic, so crossing the intersection requires steely determination. The pace, however, gives a driver sufficient time to read the hastily scrawled signs making desperate pleas: "Black Owned. Black Owned Business. Employs Black Young Mothers." Some of the messages are a bit more sinister than others: "Black Owned/Not Korean Owned"— the "O" in Korean filled with a frowning face. Tags on shells of buildings read, "It's a black thang"; little boys loot a wig store on a dare and then sport their spoils. This revolution has become cacophonous.

When I see the National Guard's Humvees I'm reminded of the passed-down memories of '65. Of the tanks that trundled authoritatively down Crenshaw, of my grandfather, in his suspenders and stingy-brimmed straw fedora, on his first visit to LA from Louisiana, wandering away. On foot, he took his own discovery trip, his expedition lasting long after curfew. He was returned to us, telling grand tales, by uniformed escort. Now I'm realizing I worry my loved ones as well, because I need to see for myself. I need to understand.

Crenshaw is now lit with a different spark. The hard-won Lucky's at the corner of 39th remains, sealed behind Alexander Haagen's trademark fence work. A Louis Farrakhan recording plays from the loudspeaker of a corner bookstore. And when about five members of the National Guard make a fast break toward 39th Street, with guns at the ready, I follow their gaze, and the tilt of their guns upraised. I see nothing, except it's the first time I notice that the sky is almost blue.

"I basically wanted to help my community," says Brandi Younger, a thirteen-year-old student at Bancroft Junior High. She's got a push broom in her hands and is working on her little piece of the Child and Adult Health Group Urgent Care building, its collapsed and untidy skeleton spilling onto the sidewalk. "I got tired of people calling us 'animals' on TV. I didn't want our community to look bad, I didn't want people to say bad things. All I've seen is looting and violence. I really haven't seen anything positive."

Lancelott Keith is taking a break when Marla Gibbs arrives with trays of catered food from her supper club, Memory Lane, to feed the crew of about fifty and growing who have gathered here with their brooms, rubber gloves, and rakes. They've come from around the corner and across town, dispatched by radio DJs, ministers, their own consciences. "Problem with the young men is that they have no work," says Keith. "No jobs. Those are the things that make you feel worthwhile. Even pushing a broom. There's been a void for too long. People have to have a purpose."

"I know people who didn't plan for the revolution," writer/performance artist Akilah Nay Oliver tells those assembled in the circle. She looks at a food-distributions list, then sends it around the room for those willing to participate to sign.

"Toilet paper and milk. Two things in a riot that go the quickest," suggests Wanda Coleman, recollecting her experience during the "old rise in '65."

Across town, a fifteen-minute freeway ride from the cleanup crews on Crenshaw, in the few hours before curfew, an ad hoc collective of black artists meets to discuss ideas for immediate relief. What comes out are the first raw emotions voiced in the first moment of calm, the public articulation of what has been swarming around everyone's brain. People wouldn't burn down something they cherish, something they perceive as truly their own. The violence of the last forty-eight hours has taken us far away from the monotone reading of the leaden verdict, the crumpled mass that was barely discernible as Rodney G. King. Now it's the stark reality of no food, of dead or absent family, of no power, of the acrid smell that clings to the clothes, the hair, the nose. "What does this signify? What kind of phoenix's gonna rise out of these particular ashes?" asks Coleman. "This didn't come out of a vacuum." "I don't want anybody to explain it in their terms," says Keith Antar Mason, barely suppressing his tears or the tremble in his voice. "This happened to me. Now it's beyond Rodney King. It's beyond 1619. There ain't no explanation for this."

"All my life I've been called an 'animal.' All my life I've been called subhuman," testifies a woman from across the room, throwing her thoughts into the circle. "We have to be careful of the language. The 'thugs,' 'rats,' 'packs,' and 'hoodlums.' I pay close attention to the words so it's been hard for me to watch TV or read the newspaper."

"If this was happening in another country, they'd talk about the repressive government," says poet Meri Nana-Ama Danquah. "Pay close attention to what these people were stealing—food, diapers, toys. No one mentioned economics."

A woman in T-shirt and jeans echoes the inchoate thought that has most occupied my own mind. "We've been trusting too long," she says quietly. "We trusted the jury to do right. I'm so mad at us for trusting..."

I'm looking out the window, listening, but thinking about the sun. About the thin light we're quickly losing, about the urgency of heading back east to beat night. I'm thinking about the collective nightmare that became our lives for hours into days, about the biblical "rainbow sign" sent after the rains, wondering how it will make itself known this time. As I drift further, what wanders in from the circle of angry voices is a stray thought, a fragment, offered up as a single puzzle piece of a larger explanation: "Maybe it had to burn...like how sometimes you have to burn a field. To make something new..."

THE CAPITAL OF AZTLAN BURNS

Adolfo Guzman Lopez

In patria chica San Diego

The llantos of Rolando Rey

Reach me at the speed of sound

Batter my swollen eyes

Electrocute

Repeatedly

Los cotorros de la televisión

Plead for reservists

To report to stations

Güera's voice oscillates

Fear

Desperation

Terror

Instinctive protection

Accorralados como bestias

Palmeras brought for 1932 Olympics

Sunglasses melt

Palm trees burn

Sol, arena, sangre

Seeping out of the streets

Of fantastic Losangelestitlán

Lined with flaming

Heretic

Palms

A pastel light of vice

Velas de luto

Around el féretro losangelino

EVERY TEN YEARS OR SO

Gar Anthony Haywood

Okay, check this out.

When LA went up in smoke and fire back in April of '92, cars burning and windows smashing and white folks ducking and diving every which way, this black man was watching all the action from what by all rights should have been ground fucking zero, the first and maybe even last place black folks should have gone to demonstrate their righteous indignation over the Rodney King non-verdict: Simi Valley. Yeah, that Simi Valley. That's where I was living at the time, though I wasn't particularly proud of it, even before the berg became internationally infamous for being home to some of the most racist and ignorant suburbanites ever to do time in a jury box.

But my homies never came to Simi. Rather than hop in the hoopty and bring their bricks and bats out to the source of all the madness, they confined their show of destruction and we-ain't-havin'-this-shit-no-more contempt for the white man's latest insult to their very humanity to the 'hood, laying waste to Vernon and Slauson and Normandie and Washington, instead of Madera Drive and Los Angeles Avenue. Cynics would say the TVs were just as good at Fedco on La Cienega and Rodeo, why the hell waste the gas?

But a reasonable man like myself could also see the wisdom in tearing shit up Five-Oh wasn't even going to try and defend, rather than so much as look cross-eyed at a fire hidrant out in Ventura County, which the local police, hell, the National Guard, would've probably used Napalm to protect.

So there I (along with the ex-wife and our two kids) sat in our Simi Valley abode, safer from all the rocks and bottles and flying glass than we had any right to be. Watching my brothers and sisters out and thinking how incredible it was that some folks were actually surprised by it all, looking upon it as they did as nothing more and nothing less than a monumental overreaction to a "controversial" courtroom verdict. I had to laugh. They hadn't seen this coming weeks ago, when the Rodney King trial was moved from LA—where a guilty verdict against the cops who beat his ass on video tape like a piñata filled with gold bullion was at least remotely possible—to Simi Valley, where damn near every third pot-bellied homeowner mowing his lawn is a badge-carrying law enforcement officer himself? Jesus, man, what world were these people living in?

When news of the non-verdict (that's right, non-verdict) broke, I was in the El Segundo office of the computer maintenance firm which employed me at the time, one of four or five technicians waiting around for our next repair call to come in. Amazingly, only I and J.B., an older white man who already feared us black folks in the every day, normal course of things, seemed to understand that our Wednesday afternoon had just changed for the worse. No one else in the office got it. While I started making plans to haul ass home, J.B. began looking around for a good place to dig a foxhole, our associates were humming about like it was business as usual, no disaster prep necessary. A trouble call came in for Dan U., a short, fortysomething nice guy of Hawaiian descent, and he was gearing up to take it. Somebody's printer was eating paper at a meat packing plant out in Vernon, and this little pale-faced doughboy was about to drive out there to fix it, blind as blind could be to the probability that the route he would have to take into Vernon was already fast becoming a war zone just looking to claim someone like him as its first victim.

But see, such was, and continues to be, the state of most people's ignorance of the black man's plight in America. Nobody ever sees our shit coming, because they aren't even aware of our constant proximity to The Edge, that precipice of insanity we are perpetually forced to teeter upon by the injustices to which we are regularly and systematically subjected. (Like being told the beating poor Rodney took under the nightsticks of four "officers of the law" was not an abomination worthy of jail time. Uh-huh.) Hence, the unenlightened react with shock, shock, mind you!, when the black man goes off every generation or so to make his injuries known, his need for justice recognized. Oblivious to the root causes of all the violence, and disproportionately appalled by the moronic vandalism that invariably accompanies it, they write our urban uprisings off as simple animal hooliganism and pray for the swift restoration of order. Political context? What political context?

It's been exactly ten years since it happened last. Life in Los Angeles for poor people of color is pretty much in the same sorry state now as it was then. Another fire is surely coming, somewhere down the road, as America's undying tolerance for racism all but guarantees. And as that dark day approaches, what I find myself wondering most of all is this:

Will my boy Dan U. be any wiser about the signs of smoke in the air this time? Or will they still take him completely by surprise?

THEY'RE GOING CRAZY OUT THERE

Erin Aubry Kaplan 79

It hardly seems possible now, nearly ten years later, that at the moment Los Angeles was setting fire to itself with the tinder of its driest and least-fed souls, I was getting a facial. It was three o'clock in the afternoon and I was reclined in a chair in an Inglewood salon, my face hot and moist and not feeling very much better than it did when I walked in roughly an hour before; but that's the beauty business, which dictates that you'll look worse before you look transformed. As I finished up, my face glowing an unnatural red, one of the salon owners came into the room and announced a little breathlessly that she'd just heard the verdicts in the Rodney King police beating case, and they were all not guilty. We were all immediately incensed—me and the owners of Le Skintique, Belinda and Regina—though not shocked. This sort of thing happens routinely and historically enough in black communities so that people are never surprised. When it happens, you renew the outrage that is about the only thing black people have passed intact from one generation to the next, outrage that is generally dormant but subcutaneous until it is activated by something like the Rodney King verdicts. The outrage got me out of that chair and moving faster than I otherwise would have—the whole point of a facial, after all, is

to relax in the aftermath—my face still flushed and raw, though now, instead of annoying it felt appropriate. Belinda and Regina empathized with Rodney King's misfortune and the whole miscarriage of justice; they shook their perfect bobs and clucked their tongues sharply. They had more customers to tend to, but they wished me well.

I went home because I didn't know where else to go, yet. During the short drive I listened to talk radio out of habit and heard, to my genuine surprise, growing pleas for calm. That could only mean that people were getting out of hand somewhere, and it was catching and irrepressible. I felt suddenly energized and maniacally happy at the idea of spontaneity, any spontaneity, overtaking a city like Los Angeles, which in my thirty years here had proven damn near impossible. It's like trying to build muscle on a long, tall frame that refuses to move quickly; the most intense exercises administered to that many square inches just don't take. Something was taking now, and though I figured it likely wasn't good, I couldn't help but marvel anyway.

When I got home the phone rang almost as soon as I walked in the door. It was a teacher friend, Ottis, who I had last seen earlier in the afternoon, not long before I went off for that facial. Ottis was a minister and a youngish veteran of the '60s civil rights movement; he had a passion for history, which is the only reason he taught a few times a week, in the adult school. He didn't need the money. He was a staunch social progressive who lectured his class constantly about the evils and futile logic of conservatism. "Girl, can you believe this?" he cried. He was clearly in his element, as energized as me. "They're going crazy out there."

He said he was going over to a rally he'd heard about happening at First AME Church, near Western and Adams. I didn't exactly like the idea of going to a church, which I knew would preach pacifism and healing—a word I would grow to hate in the decade after—more than address specifics of the verdicts and how they might actually be wrong. The problem I had with religion generally is that it accepted everything and never condemned anything as wrong, or it condemned too many things as wrong, and neither view was useful in the modern world as far as I was concerned. But I had to go somewhere, and Ottis was all charged up, and though he was a minister he would hardly stand for platitudes from Rev. Chip Murray, or anybody else. He picked me up and we drove in the bright, late-afternoon sun south towards First AME.

Going along Crenshaw I first noticed a change in the weather; the sun was the same but an unease was rising, like fog off the ocean, from the streets. It was permeable and almost invisible but it was swiftly re-ordering a landscape I had seen a thousand times before, altering it beyond emotional recognition. The closer Ottis and I got to the church, the murkier it became, until we came to a dead stop near Western and Adams because so many cars were milling about, trying to park for the rally or trying to get the hell out because the drivers sensed something bad and enveloping was afoot. For the moment we were all in suspended motion like millions of hapless atoms in a newly frozen ice cube. It felt like the odd, pristine stillness that comes before a nuclear attack or a big earthquake; the unease kept gathering like smoke as the sun beamed on. Before I could tell Ottis how anxious I was feeling, he began shouting and pointing, "Look at that!" People were wandering the streets as if the streets weren't there, filling them up with a certain defiance, shutting them down. A rough-looking man in a blue hooded sweatshirt was coming vaguely toward us, wielding a trash can. He stopped suddenly and tossed the metal can with all his might, like a javelin. That broke the cars out of their lethargy: one blond white woman in a black BMW gunned her motor, backed up with a screech and took off west down Adams, looking straight ahead the whole time, like a bat out of hell. Other people started craning their necks to determine not parking spots but points of escape; any thoughts of solidarity and Rodney King were giving way to instincts of self-preservation, which in LA means to drive, baby, drive. Ottis and I did, after sizing up the ugly mood, which was expanding before our eyes, and weighing it against going to the rally. The ugly mood won out. Neither of us said so, but we didn't want to be on foot when shit really started happening; today of all days it was probably best to follow the local creed and live out of your car if you had one. I was grateful for ours, though I had mixed feelings about the facial, about the indulgence and oblivion it stood for. It suddenly seemed impossible to argue social reform and redistributions of wealth when I was spending fifty dollars a month that I didn't really have on the promise of a surface improvement that I didn't need all that much, and wasn't likely to happen anyway. The fire on my face had cooled, the incriminating evidence for the moment gone. I was relieved.

Ottis and I headed west and didn't stop until we hit Brentwood. I don't know why we traveled that far; I suppose we wanted to ensure our escape from the haunted forest of South LA and its roiling clouds of discontent to the bright Oz of somewhere else. Those distinctions of place were usually clear, but not today. Brentwood was nice, but it could blow too. Our energy high had broken down to a kind of gray nervousness that lacked the romance of three o'clock. We knew the city was burning now, and where. We sat in a Brentwood bar with a smattering of white people who preferred to watch a Lakers game on television than tune in to the news. Ottis and I fairly reared up in indignation, loudly deploring the apathy of certain people in this city, and believed our own indignation. The white people looked mildly ashamed but said nothing, returning to their drinks. We had the floor. To these folks we were not sellouts or deserters but emissaries of conscience, unwelcome, sure, but loud, eloquent voices of condemnation and reason; we represented. We couldn't quite face the rally but we could do this, here, all day long. We were good at it. The streets, we learned that day, were not our pulpit. That was the fallen altar for the faithless, the pulpit of an old imagination, the province of pitifully angry people with trash barrels and nowhere to throw them. We had new havens—mahogany bars, spas, salons—in which to forge the future. We had grudging audiences but transformation was still in our hands. To say nothing of our faces.

ON CALL

Victoria Gutierrez-Kovner

In 1992, I worked for a rape victim counseling services agency. The shifts were 24-hours long. The on-call shift was once a month from 5 p.m. until 8 p.m.

The night of April 29th, I was on-call. The clearest memory I have of that night was literally going back and forth to the hospital my entire shift. Since I was so busy, at one point I decided to stay until the next morning. Of all my years of doing this, this was the one night that really stands out.

There were five rape victims that night: One was a child.

Early in my shift, before I was aware of what was occurring in the city, I assisted a rape victim and then went home. A few hours later, I had to go back again. Two of the rapes happened in the area where the rioting occurred. These victims were homeless women.

The first time I went home after counseling a victim, my husband didn't want me to go back. But of course I had to. It was eerie driving to the hospital and felt very unsafe. Unlike reports on TV of clamoring crowds, the freeway was empty and completely smoked over.

My husband followed me in his car. Typically, it's a 15-minute drive, but it took much longer than that. Our regular route wasn't available, because police were blockading exits and streets. It was dark and sirens erupted out of everywhere. I feared for my husband driving back home and made him promise to call when he returned safely.

I wonder if September 11th was similar. The media underscored the many out-of-control types of behaviors, yet the individuals I worked with really stepped up to assist and take the role of helper. People really put aside their own fears and feelings of helplessness when there are others in greater need. On the night of April 29th, I found myself counseling not only the rape victims, but also the staff of the hospital. While it felt like a safe house in one respect, the employees needed a lot of follow-up counseling to regain their sense of confidence. My own fears were supplanted by a feeling of contribution. While I couldn't change the outcome of that night for the women I counseled, I could offer them companionship and a belief that, in the midst of all this chaos, was a helping hand.

FROM FIRELIGHT

Larry Kronish

In this excerpt from Larry Kronish's novel, *Firelight*, Brian, fourteen, is telling his sister Beaty, eleven, what he has just seen on TV.

"You shoulda seen em, Beaty, you shoulda seen em. There was this guy outside this liquor store and he picked up this big metal Marlboro sign, you know the kind they put out to hang the price on? He picked up this big metal Marlboro sign and smashed it into this car window. And this other guy, he had like a car jack, and he's smashing it in the front window of this other car and then he runs around to the driver's side and smashes that window and then starts like punching this driver in the car. And then there's this other car and they set this car on fire, right in this gas station and then it rolls halfway out into the street so it's half in the driveway and half in the street and this fire's just rushing out of its windows."

Brian's voice gets real quiet and says, "I think there was someone in it. He like was burning to death. If you weren't black…they pulled this truck driver…I mean he was driving along the street in this huge truck except that it was so crazy and people were running back and forth in the street and smashing cars, and they pulled him out of his truck and they were smashing him, smashing his head kicking him.

And he was just lying there on the ground and this guy maybe he was twenty or something, I don't know, this guy walked over to him and threw this brick down right on the white guy's head. I mean he threw it hard! And then this guy, the guy that threw the brick, he like does this dance after he smashes him, dance like an Egyptian kinda, all you know like I'm fuckin' bad. And the truck driver is like lying on the ground and you can see that he's like really hurt. And every time the truck driver gets up somebody smashes him again. And finally like, somehow, he crawls to his truck and starts driving it, and there's like cars in the streets like it's some kinda war zone. And people are running all over the place. And there's fires and smoke going up in the air. And there's people breaking into the stores and stealin' stuff, armfuls of stuff, and like mobs of people. You shoulda seen it Beaty. They're goin' crazy."

"I don't want to see it," I say.

"Why'd they let em go? Why'd they find em not guilty? I can't fucking believe it. That's so racist. You saw it, didn't 'cha. You saw those cops fuckin' him up. Why'd they let em go? I never seen nothing like this, Beaty. There's all these people Downtown, in fronta the police building. And it's like, 'No justice no peace.' And people screamin' and giving the cops the finger and throwin' rocks at em and bottles and stuff. And the cops with like shields and helmets and batons. And the cops are scared, you can see it. And the people are like…I think they're gonna fuckin' riot Downtown, Beaty." And Brian looks at me again, not just looking at me but like how can you tell when someone's really serious and Brian is really serious and he says, "What if they come here, Beaty!"

And I say, my heart pounding up against my chest and like I can see them running up along the River up out of Chinatown, this big shadowy mob of arms and legs and screams and fires and, "What makes you think they're gonna come here? Why would they come here?"

"Cuz they're going everywhere," Brian says. "You didn't see em, Beaty. You shoulda seen em. I never seen nothing like this before."

"But why would they come here?" I say, my voice screeching in my throat. "We don't hurt anybody. Why would they come here? Why are they mad at us?"

Brian just stares out like he's looking at the ivy, but he's not. He's like just staring, at the people, like they're coming. And he says, "I don't think they're mad at us, Beaty. I think they're just mad, and we're white, you know? They're mad and we're white. When I was in there, Grandma Alice called, and she was like screaming, 'They're coming up the freeway! They're coming up the streets! They're coming, they're coming, they're gonna burn Pasadena!' And like there's nothing on TV about it but she's screaming."

Firelight takes places on April 29, 1992, from about 7:00 a.m. to 11:00 p.m. A series of first-person narratives follows the Turlei family who are white: father DT, son Brian-fourteen, daughter Beaty (Beatrice)-eleven, and two of their neighbors, Mrs. Ngo—a Vietnamese woman in her eighties—and Mr. Cutler—a black man in his seventies—through the events of the day. This excerpt is from Chapter 29, "Beaty," where Brian describes the outbreak at Florence and Normandie, the beating of Reginald Denny, and other moments from the first hours of the riots as Brian saw it on TV.

On the Saturday three days after the riots began, I drove to the First AME Church in South Central with several friends, fellow parents at my son's preschool, hoping to be of some small help in cleaning up the devastation. It was unclear to us how safe it was for three carloads of white liberals from the west side to be in the area or how we would be received, but it was also clear that to just sit and watch whatever happened on TV was to declare that we were not part of a larger community.

As it turned out, we were hardly alone. A couple of blocks before we reached the church, we joined a slow long line of cars filled with people from all over Los Angeles. Like us, they brought food and clothes and water that church members gladly helped to unload. When we were done, we were welcomed by men with walkie-talkies who were in contact with colleagues at various clean-up areas, who told them how many people were needed there. We said we were willing to do whatever was asked and were sent to the remnants of a fire a couple of miles away.

The scenery on the drive looked no different than any war zone of the moment. Power lines were down, buildings on every block were burned. Traffic lights were out but amidst the destruction there was a veneer of calm. Cars moved orderly and calmly. No horns, no speeding, no crowding. We came to a corner where two large buildings still smoldered, a small fire still sizzling in one. The roofs had collapsed, the windows were gone, nothing had survived—except the huge ficus trees at the curb six feet away, standing tall and green by the boulevard.

The sidewalk was covered with charred debris. Fifty people—black, white, Latino—swept and shoveled and lugged away the rubble. No one talked much except the guys struggling with the huge pieces, and our talk was about only the best way to proceed with our job. Only after a long while did I realize that I had no idea what the people I had been standing shoulder-to-shoulder with for half an hour looked like. I knew their knees and backs and hands, but not their faces. In a remarkably short time we had cleared the sidewalk and moved on to the next building, which was cleared just as fast, and then we were directed to another intersection and started again. I don't pretend to think that our labor made much difference. All we did was pile burned stuff on more burned stuff that had to be bulldozed and cleared away so something new could be built, but I like to think that the symbolic effort was useful.

Next to one place we worked a woman whose beauty shop was spared stood in her doorway and offered us water and a toilet. As we stood there, three guys in their 20s hooted and jeered as they drove by in a new red BMW that I doubt they bought with money saved from their paper routes. After they had passed a man across the street with a shopping cart sparsely filled with Coke cans and other small things that he could salvage in return for a few bucks stopped and looked over at us.

"Tell me, where are we going to buy food?" he shouted. "Where are we going to get clothes? We don't need you and your brooms. We need food." Disgusted, he turned and continued on.

After a few hours we were sent to the main staging area, a cluttered corner lot which until three days ago was a shopping center, where we were told there was nothing more for the day. We were eager to return to our children but we also didn't want to leave. It was still light and it seemed that there should be other jobs to do. A crew that had been working there finished loading a dumpster with metal debris, then quit for the day and joined. Soft drinks and sandwiches donated by someone were handed out. We all talked quietly as we ate and drank and slowly realized that we were quite tired. Presently we noticed that there were other people around. A group offering to register people to vote was doing a little business in one corner of the lot, and as were getting ready to drive home, some Hare Krishnas arrived and set up their tambourines across the street. For the briefest, the very briefest of moments, it was almost as if everything was all right.

ARSENIO AND THE MAYOR

Peter Maunu 93

I had the good fortune, for over five years, to play my music with a great group of people on a nationally syndicated show—The Arsenio Hall Show. It was an important moment in television history, a racially mixed show that catered to a culturally diverse audience. I was the whitest guy in the band, but it didn't really matter since musicians are, for the most part, colorblind.

The night the city burned, it was business as usual, but not really, on the Paramount Lot. There was definitely a sense of calm before the storm: The studio was at the Melrose and La Brea area, which was temporarily a quiet oasis while around us the city began to burn.

The show taped at 5 p.m. and the verdicts had come down earlier that afternoon. Almost instantly the city was in an uproar. I don't know how I heard that we were going on, but somehow I managed to get to the lot. Everyone was in shock about the verdicts, and already there were isolated incidents of looting and riots. Reginald Denny had already been pulled from his rig and beaten.

How do you do the Arsenio Hall Show, with a big, celebratory, party atmosphere, after the verdicts? I found it courageous that

Arsenio went on with his show that day rather than do a rerun, which no one would have faulted him for. It was really difficult to know what to say since, strangely, no one was prepared for what should be said.

That night Mayor Tom Bradley came on the show. It was a great venue for Bradley, the demographics were largely black and it had a national reach. Rather than the usual couches the show used, Hall and Bradley sat on stools facing the cameras. Maybe there was a live studio audience that night, but I don't remember one. I know there was no band that night: I was sitting in the audience box, watching the show instead of on the bandstand playing.

There was much discussion about the role of the media and what was appropriate to show and discuss on TV before the taping. During the show Arsenio and the mayor talked about damage control—already the print media were editorializing the situation in terms of black vs. white, them vs. us. There was a lot of discussion about Martin Luther King Jr. It really felt as though these words of nonviolence were being fed to us by our two black leaders, the odd couple of Arsenio and Bradley, to keep the peace, whereas Dr. King himself would have had something more substantial to say in that situation. There was little talk of injustice and no talk of the inequities of our city, but it was Paramount—I guess you can't get too controversial on their dollar.

I remember Arsenio talking to Bradley using lots of quotes from Martin Luther King. I get tired, personally, of hearing the words of King used to keep the peace or the status quo. Primarily he was an activist. In times of great social injustice, he would have had an idea of where to go. I felt sorry for both Bradley and Arsenio, who obviously wanted to say something to soothe the city, but couldn't find their own words.

I turned to my bandmate, bassist John B. (Williams), and said, "I keep hearing so much about what Dr. King would be saying. What about Malcolm X?" He shrugged. It was obvious that we were being fed only part of the story.

I remember the Kennedy assassination and watching my dad come home with tears in his eyes, normally my dad never cried. During the uprising I didn't cry either, but that night it felt as though my world was turned upside down.

I could tell that Bradley's words were not going to have much of an effect. He might have been a great leader in his time, but it was obvious that his time was past. There were definitely studio constraints as to what could be said, so we'll never really know what message they wanted to get across. But I left the show disappointed at a missed opportunity.

When we finished the show it was still light out. Normally, I got out of there about 6:30 or so. There was smoke everywhere and no one was on the freeway, those Berlin Walls that carve up the city's neighborhoods.

Things became more divisive in Hollywood after the riots. Arsenio became the black show and Leno and Letterman were the white shows. It became the way the shows were packaged. Arsenio didn't last much longer after that. Neither did Bradley, for that matter.

THE ANTI-HEROS: THE LA4

Donna Mungen

While all eyes turned on the second Rodney King trial, others whispered and waited to see if Los Angeles would explode again should the verdict not be well received in certain neighborhoods.

Meanwhile, little media attention was being paid to the trial of the LA4: four young black men who made video history on the catastrophic afternoon of April 29, 1992 as truck driver Reginald Denny made his ill-fated turn into the heart of South Central LA and the eye of a brewing social storm.

Even though most LA residents (both within and outside of the black community) reviled the actions of the young men known as the LA4, they still had a small faithful contingent of supporters who held a rally during the court proceedings. The event erupted into a near mini-riot before it was quickly extinguished by the forceful presence of the police, and I had the fortune to be there that day.

I stopped and queried a young female demonstrator regarding her reasoning and motivation for supporting the LA4's dastardly deeds. She turned to me with fiery eyes and barked back, "I don't think what the officers did to Rodney King was fair, and I don't think what these guys did is fair either. But if the white officers can get off, why can't these brothers get off? I feel there should be justice for black men as there is for white men."

For many Angelenos, the image of the televised dawn raid of Chief Darryl Gates, decked out in his warrior bullet-proofed vest, arresting the most notorious of the defendants: Damien 'Football' Williams remains singed to their eye filaments. According to the indictments served that day, Williams was charged with making an acrobatic fly-kick to the skull of the semi-conscious Reginald Denny who lay sprawled defenselessly in the middle of the street.

The four defendants later had the book thrown at them and were slapped with exorbitant bails. Legal tactics succeeded in getting some of the charges rescinded, but even the ones that stuck promised to keep all four of them on 'ice' for the rest of their natural lives.

As an armchair attorney, I found the legal disparities between the treatment of the defendants in the King and Denny cases quite disturbing. From inception, the police officers were released on bail (which allowed some enough time to publish their own sensational accounts of the original Rodney King assault). And even during the most heated days of the King trial, the consequences of a 'guilty' verdict for the police officers never included prospects that they would never see the light of day. However, all efforts at plea-bargaining in the LA4 case were rejected, and repeated accusations of racism reinforced by previous judicial decisions involving African-American defendants only served to compromise the public's perception of the government's case against the LA4.

Yet among most of my friends, few, if any, found much to champion in the LA4 case. This was no "Free Angela Davis" or "Down With the Pigs" political cause celeb. I'd go as far to say these young men were anti-heroes, or as the president of local branch of the NAACP announced at the time, "there are plenty of others you can find every day who are more appropriate to defend."

In a perverse way, the actions of the LA4 represented not only a lost generation, but also the worst that the African-American community had to offer. They were not the reason we marched on Washington in 1963, nor did their actions proclaim, "I am somebody." Rather 'they were the ones we wished to forget.'

Still they were our children, and we were forced to consider them and their actions. It has been said: You can't always love the deeds of your children. As much as I dislike the alleged actions of the LA4, I couldn't just completely dismiss the woman demonstrator's remarks. Certainly the actions of these young men were partially the manifestation of many of the problems brewing inside of our urban cookers. But the lingering question was how we could make succeeding generations of Black men feel it was not necessary to kick a White man in the head in order to obtain a measure of self-esteem.

The legal playing field must be leveled so that the reality of any case, including such high-profile cases such as the LA4, Rodney King, or several years later the O.J. Simpson trial, demonstrate that everyone can obtain equal justice. I think it is no accident that both of these cases occurred at the same time. They served as a Yin and Yang influence in America—the ebb and flow—of life. We are forced, whether we like it or not, to look at the flip side of the coin and somehow, if we don't have to burn down and destroy the place we live to the essence of the truth, maybe we can be better from the process.

After 1992, the image of LA moved from one of the most desirable American cities to the home of increased unemployment, business flight, racial bigotry, drive-by shootings, and high foreclosure rates. And if that wasn't enough, we had the very dark apocalyptic concept further reinforced with the release of the movie *Falling Down*, the story of an mentally disturbed, unemployed engineer, played by Michael Douglas, who is mad as hell and isn't going to take it anymore, which visually translated into him going on a rampage kicking the asses of Koreans, Mexicans, women, and gays.

So little of these images reflect the love and beauty that has brought over 13 million residents from all corners of the world to live in LALA land. There's more to this city of rainbow faces, instant beach culture, constantly moving geography, and too often polluted vistas.

The other day I was thinking that when the East Coast seems like it would never surface from the 'Snow of the Century,' that I'd rather take my chances here with eighty degree days. Indeed, LA's been bruised, scarred, and shaken to its roots, but we're only two hundred years old—sort of like a preteen with a major outbreak of acne. And in spite of the anti-heroes, there is still a lot of wonderful stuff here, and will continue to remain home for many Angels.

I was a member of the California National Guard in 1992. I was twenty-three years old and finishing my second semester of college. I was married and my wife was six months pregnant. To make ends meet, I was working security full time at the closest hotel to LAX. At the time I had been out of the active duty Army for two years.

On April 29, I was working my usual 3:00 to 11:00 p.m. shift. There was a lot of commotion in the building because the Rodney King verdicts were coming down the pipeline. Many people talked about being surprised. I wasn't! For days people in the hotel talked about what could happen if the cops were set free. Those that lived in South Central knew that violence would erupt in their neighborhoods. It seems that the only ones without a clue were law enforcement agencies.

It should've been obvious. How could they expect people to casually accept the verdicts without a revolt? The whole world saw a man beaten needlessly within inches of his life! Anyone in their right mind was able to see this on the video. Only a cop-loving jury would find them innocent. That's why the trial was moved to Simi Valley.

As soon as the verdicts came in, I went to the employee lounge to talk to the people gathered there to watch the verdicts on television.

I found the lounge almost full. Many were yelling at the TV in anger. An elderly African-American woman was crying.

The people were still arguing when the program was interrupted by a special report on "buildings that were burning in South Central LA." It was soon followed by helicopter coverage of the mayhem at the Corner of Florence and Normandie.

The violence at Florence and Normandie was shocking to say the least. An African-American mob had gathered. They began throwing bottles at cars. Some of the cars crashed and the occupants were pulled out and beaten. Most of those beaten were Latinos who found themselves in the wrong place at the wrong time. It was during the televised beatings that a character named "Football" bounced a brick off trucker Reginald Denny's head.

My moment of truth came around 7:00 p.m. when I received a call from a staff Sergeant in my National Guard unit. He said that we had been activated and that I was to report to my armory as soon as possible. I said good-bye to my co-workers and hello to the deadliest riots of the 20th Century.

At home, I found it tough to say goodbye to my pregnant wife. She had gathered all that I would need for the next few days and was an emotional wreck. She cried through the entire fifteen minutes that I was there. I understood how she felt, but I didn't feel so good myself, going out to protect others while leaving my wife at home to protect herself.

Getting to the Inglewood Armory was quite a mission. It took me a half an hour to get there, even though I lived only five minutes away. It was crazy! People were ignoring lights and stop signs in their urgency to get home. A lady almost ran in to me as she ran a stop sign.

When I got to the armory, all I found were several scared officers and a couple of nervous sergeants, most were active duty guard members. I was the lowest ranked man (a specialist) so they handed me a loaded M-16 and they told me to watch the parking gate. I would be there until almost two in the morning. During this time almost 150 cars came through the gate. Most soldiers had horror stories to tell about what they had seen on their way there. (One soldier's car had been shot with a .357 Magnum. The bullet had gone through the trunk, the back seat, front seat, and the dash. It had vanished somewhere in the engine compartment. Luckily the driver was unscathed.)

That morning we didn't get a rest until 3:00 a.m. The lights went out and we were told to sleep. How could we sleep?! Our back yards were burning. Most of us lived in, or very close to, the areas in chaos. In the darkness you could hear nervous conversations as we anxiously waited for orders to hit the street.

The lights were out for only a couple of hours. When they came on the building burst to life. A formation was called, an inspection was done, and a promise was made that we would be in the streets shortly. This promise would not be kept for unknown reasons. This would weigh on the conscience of all of us for a long time.

It would be more than a day before we would leave that armory. In the meantime, about two hundred of us were kept cooped up until most of the rioting had died down. It was frustrating as we sat back doing meaningless tasks while part of our city went down in flames.

Almost ten years have passed and I still feel the wounds of the people that lost their businesses or livelihoods because of the riots. First the police let them down by failing to take action at Florence and Normandie. We failed by sitting back twirling our thumbs. Somebody should've paid for holding us back. I think Pete Wilson, the former governor, should have been held responsible.

As we waited for the order to move out. We pulled guard duty, cleaned weapons, and talked a lot. At the same time a mob formed a block away from the armory and proceeded to burn down our favorite 7-11 store and an auto-parts store. I saw a sergeant so angry because he couldn't leave the armory to help that his eyes swelled with tears.

Late in the second night of the riots our unit finally moved out. The company was taken by Deuce and a Half trucks (heavy-duty 2.5 ton trucks used by the military) to the city of Lynwood, about five miles away. My guard unit was the first one to hit the streets; soon the whole city would be crawling with National Guard, active Army, and Marines. The trip to Lynwood was quite interesting. We passed by a few buildings that were still on fire. One of these was a Payless shoe store where, a week before, I had bought my wife's shoes. Next to the shoe store was a small market where a uniformed officer was holding a shotgun on an assortment of probable gang members who hugged the floor.

Near Lynwood on Imperial Highway, we passed a brutal fight where five people seemed to be in a life and death struggle. As we passed, they stopped the brawl and stared at us, as if they expected us to arrest them. When we kept going they went back to their fight. The scene was so surreal; it seemed like something out a cartoon.

We set up our headquarters in the city of Lynwood. Our base was a sheriff's youth building. It had a nice boxing ring. We would spend the next ten days there. Here we were issued forty rounds and sent out into the streets. We left quickly; it would be forty-eight hours before we would see our gear again.

After we left our headquarters, my thirty-man platoon spent the first two days going from one place to the next. We covered areas of Lynwood, Compton, and Watts. Sometimes we patrolled, at other times we set up a perimeter around areas that had already been looted. In some places we spent only a few hours, in others we spent the night. We slept less than a total of four hours in those two days.

It was in one of those perimeters where I had my most unforget-table experience. In the city of Lynwood, a fellow soldier and I were covering the rear parking lot of a looted store. We had set up a wooden barricade that led to a blocked off street. It was about two in the morning when a speeding car came out of the blocked off street and ran over our barricade. It barely missed us as it went into the rear parking lot. There was no way out so the car turned around and headed toward us.

My partner, who had never seen anything violent, proceeded to get in front of the car and aim his weapon at the driver. He then froze when the vehicle went toward him, his face turned pale in the headlights. The vehicle stopped and the driver gunned the engine. The car didn't move, it must have been in neutral. I think the driver expected my partner to get out of the way so that he could get out of there. To tell the truth, so did I.

The standoff lasted only a couple of seconds. I realized that my partner wasn't going to move. He was frozen in fear. I yelled at the driver not to move and ran toward him. I stopped only a couple of feet from him and aimed at his head. I asked him to turn off the engine. I was relieved when he did.

He looked like a hard-core gang member with tattoos and a shaved head. Next to him sat an attractive young woman who began to weep. We let them go, we could've held them for running over our barricades or violating curfew. But we were just happy that nothing happened. I still wonder if the gang member ever realized how close he came to dying that night. It would've happened in a fraction of a second. If he would have stepped on the accelerator I would've fired without a second thought.

In retrospect, one of the most important lessons that I gathered is that a person needs to have a plan to protect his or her family in a time of chaos. During the riots I talked to many victims of crime. I learned that they were victims largely because they could not protect themselves. In most instances they called the police and the police never responded.

One aspect of the disturbance that confounds me is the official death count. It is my belief that the official count was a little over fifty. Yet from conversations with sheriff's deputies and security officers, I believe that it could be much higher.

One specific instance that really stands out is with a couple of security officers during the riots. They swore that they had killed two gang members. I asked some of the local shop owners and they verified the story. Another conversation I had was with a couple of sheriff's deputies who bragged that their SWAT team had killed a couple of snipers. I was never able to verify this, but other sources knew about the snipers killed by the sheriffs. Were they counted?

Later I read a newspaper account of all the deaths that happened as a direct result of the riots. I couldn't find these accounts. Could these stories have been made up? It's also possible that the death count was kept down to minimize the severity of the events.

And what about the nonviolent deaths that occurred? My platoon sergeant (a wonderful person) never reported to the armory because he died of a heart attack the first night of the riots. How many others must have died in a similar way? Personally, I feel that they all should be counted, after all, their deaths happened "as a result of the riots."

As the ten-year anniversary approaches I wonder if we have learned anything. Police methods haven't changed much. The Rampart scandal makes the Rodney King beating look like child's play.

Today if you drive down most riot-damaged areas you will find plenty of empty lots. Many businesses were never rebuilt. The people still live in the same conditions as before. The socioeconomic status of most neighborhoods has not changed. I ask myself, can it happen again? Why not? It's happened before.

ABSTRACTED

Kristin L. Petersen

Saturday, May 2, 1992

There we were. Two seventeen-year-old blonds from middle-class families in Pasadena, pinned. Stiff as we moved up and down, lifting charred pieces of wood, chunks of liquor bottles, and shattered flower vases from a florist shop and liquor store at the burnt down northeast corner of Allen and Villa, on the east side of Pasadena. *Keep cleaning. Whitey. This is all your fault.* Disembodied voices. Drifting from low riders that I only watched out of the corner of my eye. They circled the block twice, three times. I lost count as I tried to ignore them. Not looking up, afraid to make eye contact and connect. Afraid our parents were right. It was better to hide inside until the smoke blew out to the desert, with the windows closed and blinds drawn to the perpetually sunny LA days.

I'd had the luxury to not need to see myself in racial terms until the Riots. The pipe dream of a color-blind society. The same way almost ten years later I had not often thought of myself as American until September 11, 2001. The indulgence of not being forced to think of myself in a historical context, a political context, an economic context, a racial and ethnic context. The luxury of ignorance.

The world beyond my immediate personal circle of friends, family, and acquaintances whom I knew individually; the world in which I blurred into a symbol.

Rodney King lived in Altadena. He had gone to John Muir High School. My mom was born in Altadena. She too had gone to John Muir. So had Jackie Robinson. He went to Muir in the 1930s, at a time when Pasadena enforced restrictive convenance laws barring blacks from buying homes in white areas of the city. Jackie never returned to the city that ignored his older brother Mack's achievement of nearly beating Jesse Owens at the 1936 Olympics. Mack remained in northwest Pasadena all of his life, pressuring the city to honor Jackie. In 1997, shortly before Mack's death, Pasadena unveiled nine-foot-tall bronze busts of both brothers, situated across the street from City Hall.

I was born in Pasadena in 1974, the decade after Civil Rights and Women's Lib, into what I was told was a more civilized, evolved world. But the same people were still alive. People don't change their views and beliefs that quickly.

And the Los Angeles of the 1990s was far more ethnically and culturally diverse than ever in its history.

Wednesday, April 29, 1992

I, like everyone I knew, was shocked by the verdict. I had seen the videotape.

I was angry.

My dad was driving back to LA from the Bay Area. He stopped at a rest stop along the 5 after he heard the news. He cautioned us to stay inside. I was annoyed at his over-protectiveness. I did not need a parent to keep me inside—the chaos unfolding on TV was enough to keep me glued to the living room floor, staring at the images, and occasionally walking outside the house to smell the fires.

I hoped school would be closed the next day. A day off would be nice.

Thursday, April 30, 1992

Our high school was at Cal State LA, on the border of East LA and Alhambra. The Los Angeles County High School for the Arts, the LA version of "Fame," where I was a visual arts major in my junior year. Privileged to dedicate our days to creative pursuits at a college campus instead of a standard high school. Taking our liberal politics for granted—you can't be a creative type without vowing to become a Democrat upon age eighteen. Naïve to think that since our public high school was ethnically diverse, with students from every corner of LA County, that we did not have to examine our assumptions. We just were creative, of course. No racial conflicts here.

Thursday morning I was called out of English class to the school's attendance office in King Hall at Cal State LA. My mom was on the phone. There was a fire at the Sears at Foothill and Michillinda, just a few blocks away from my house in east Pasadena. She warned me to be careful on the drive home.

Later that afternoon, we were quarantined. Quarantined teenagers. The only time I'd heard that term before was in reference to the Mediterranean Fruit Fly quarantine on backyard fruit, barring you from transporting homegrown oranges across town. We were ordered to sit in supervised groups on the lawn outside of King Hall. As the afternoon progressed, the smell of fires grew stronger, the sky a glassy smoke that stung the lungs, harsher than the perpetual layer of smog that floated over Cal State LA, obscuring the San Gabriel Mountains.

Suddenly, we were evacuated. Bomb threats, we were told. The entire campus had thirty minutes left to evacuate. Since I had blond hair, some "well-meaning" elder at the school warned that I keep it covered as I drove home. Do not make eye contact.

I shrugged them off as silly bigots.

As we left Cal State LA, kids lingered in Lot F, trading rumors. Snipers on the 5! Someone with a gun on Fremont St.! Looting! Real history in the making.

And we were at our prime, teenagers in high school who thought we were already adults. Turning on the television, watching crowds burst open windows, leave with arms overflowing with stuff. One huge shopping spree. No rules.

Saturday, May 2, 1992

My best friend Courtney, a fellow art student, and I drove to the corner of Allen and Villa in East Pasadena, the one major site of fire in Pasadena. Of over 5,550 fires set in LA during the Riots, thirteen were in Pasadena. Of the thirteen, this one had caused the most damage. I had brought my camera. I was self-conscious of my attempt to record, document, memorialize. And material for my photography class while I was at it. Maybe I would get an A.

I wore flip-flops on the warm Spring afternoon. I had thought I would remain at a distance in my car, or tip-toe on the periphery.

I focused my lenses on the corner liquor store. One lone bottle of Southern Comfort sat on the counter, nearly untouched amid the shattered bottles on the former shelves.

Then the owners of the stores arrived. We were poking around the burnt out stores, stepping gingerly on the damaged goods, looking for the most interesting angles for photos. Our souvenirs. Their loss. They told us to leave, or at least help them clean up.

Courtney and I agreed to help.

We did not exchange introductions.

They handed us shovels and pointed towards the plastic trash cans. I alternated taking close-up pictures of the burnt wood frame buildings and scooping up crap with the shovels. Picture, shovel, picture, shovel. Scraping the shovel against the concrete and linoleum floors. The warm sun blared down through the missing roofs.

After twenty minutes bits of glass were falling between my toes. I drove home quickly to put on boots and work clothes. I rushed out of the house before my parents could ask me what I was up to. I left my camera in the car when I returned.

We continued to help the strangers clean for most of the afternoon, shifting rubble around and clearing out the skeletons of the buildings. What was the point? Someone would still have to bulldoze the structure and rebuild from scratch. Didn't they have heavy machinery designed for this task, more efficient than shovels?

Then the cars drove by, slowly. We felt the eyes on us, but did not look up. We were aligned with business owners we did not know. By helping, we moved from observers to participants. And we could be hated for what that action symbolized. We had to accept that responsibility.

Monday, May 4, 1992

When we were allowed back to school after the weekend, rumors cruised non-stop through the King Hall corridors. Some kid had been forced to sleep over night at the RTD station, another had been stuck at the campus, since his South LA neighborhood was burning and he had no way to get home. A friend who lived in Crenshaw, the only white Catholic family on the block, had a window of his mom's car shot out. The Crenshaw strip, Koreatown, Pico Boulevard., Olympic Boulevard—charcoaled structures and shards of glass. Kids bragged about the loot they procured—stereos, TVs, cameras, food.

I was a member of the student council. Our president was then-LA City Council Woman Jackie Goldberg's niece, a fabulously outspoken and confident liberal, destined to follow in her aunt's political footsteps. We had a discussion just to vent and talk about where we had been, what our stories were. One girl who was black talked about friends who looted and the fires she watched. One girl who was Korean talked about how her family stood guard on top of their store in Koreatown, armed with loaded guns. Both girls had been friends of mine, of each other. Suddenly, they were just black girl and Korean girl, and Korean girl started to cry as black girl yelled at her about Korean store owners.

All of the pent up anger and tension exploded and the riots were equally personal and impersonal, as individual frustrations, pain, and injustices came together with something larger. Peace was fragile. We were like a huge family, arguing and distrustful.

Suddenly the comments that in the past had been whispered or held silent were spoken. Like invisible earthquake faults that suddenly make themselves visible after toppling a freeway overpass, or splitting a fissure in the earth.

Weeks later in a painting class, a student brought in painting he'd done off the fires as he saw them on his TV. Large 20"x30" canvasses coated in clumps of orange, yellow, red, and black acrylic paint. He painted the frames to look like television cabinets, with knobs to turn the channel. He explained that the fires looked to him like the pastoral bonfires of ancient tribes. Pretty and detached, like the video game-style images of the 1991 Gulf War on CNN.

The photos I took of the burnt stores became part of the portfolio that got me accepted into every art school I applied to. My reflections on the riots were the subject matter for my application essays. To East Coast colleges, the Riots were exotic and confirmed many stereotypes about our apocalyptic megalopolis.

I did not get a single rejection letter.

I had forgotten that at least sixty people died. Ten years later I look at the *L.A. Times* I had saved from April 30 and May 1, 1992. A decade later it looks just ugly and complicated.

After the Riots, at least some people started to acknowledge the real anger and the complexity of the city. The event forced us to face that racial and economic conflicts in this city were no longer black vs. white, as the Watts Riots of the 1960s were perceived. The newspapers identified everyone with a racial tag, at differing levels of detail. White, black, brown. Korean. Japanese. Mexican. Latino. Chicano. African-American. Anglo. Hispanic. Zooming in and out on varying degrees of specificity and political resonance, yet ultimately all abstractions. Individuals blurred into tribal associations based on skin color, with economic divisions and conflicts at the roots. Our past knowledge faded and fear and anger prevailed—we could not process individual identities, our eyes blurred in the smoke. We saw abstractions.

Just like the photos I took. They could be of arson damage anywhere in the world, at any time. You can't even tell what type of business it was. Who owned it. How they got there and why. Who lived around there? Who patronized it? Was it a crime of opportunity, or politically informed rage?

I did not know. It was just a shape and a color, and shades of gray.

THE SOUNDS OF STRUGGLE:
Looking Back on the 1992 Los Angeles Uprising Through Music

Robert D. Peterson

"*If sometime our great artists have been the most critical of our society, it is because of their sensitivity and their concern for justice, which must motivate any true artist, makes them aware that our nation falls short of its highest potential. I see little of more importance to the future of our country and our civilization than full recognition of the place of the artist.*"—John F. Kennedy, 1963, while speaking at a small ceremony at Amherst College in honor of Robert Frost.

By examining music we can delve into the multileveled lives and struggles of Los Angeles communities and residents. And in the examination of the 1992 Los Angeles Uprising, music is even more useful in understanding its impact on our city. There have been musical depictions of the Uprising by bands such as Sublime in their song "April 29, 1992." But we can also see the effects of the Uprising on music today, music created by young musicians influenced by their experiences of the Uprising in their teenage years.

The Uprising was a turning point for many young LA musicians, who were just beginning to define their artistic and life directions. There was a realization that the current techniques of struggle were not effective and that music could become a tool for struggle. A musical community of consciousness led by bands such as Ozomatli and Quetzal was formed, in many ways as a response to the Uprising. Musicians have taken it upon themselves to organize for the empowerment of their communities. For as William Faulkner said in his acceptance speech for the Nobel prize for literature, "The poet's voice need not merely be the record of man. It can be one of the props, the pillars to help him endure and prevail."

In the thirty years preceding this Uprising, the demographic face of Los Angeles was radically transformed. In 1960, eight out of every ten Los Angeles County residents was white. Over the next thirty years, Hispanic and Asian populations grew while the white population dwindled. Unlike patterns in prior decades, increases in the black population did little to alter the ethnic mix. In many neighborhoods in South Los Angeles blacks were leaving—opening the door for new Latino immigrants. Racial transition in neighborhoods was no longer a black and white issue. Latinos, Asians, Armenians, among others, were changing the face of Los Angeles. This emerging demographic diversity is only the beginning of a fundamental rethinking of America's identity and culture. By 2056, most Americans will trace their descent to Africa, Asia, Central America, South America, the Pacific Islands, Arabia—almost anywhere but white Europe. This demographic transformation is the backdrop to understanding the '92 Uprising and the musicians who responded to it.

The factors that led to the riots are varied—police brutality, housing segregation, economic injustice. A boiling kettle of rage had been created. This anger was poignantly described by Los Angeles rap artist Ice Cube. In the midst of Du Soon Ja's[1] conviction and sentencing in late 1991, Ice Cube issued a brutal judgment of his own in his song "Black Korea":

"Pay respect to the black fist or we'll burn your store right down to a crisp, and then we'll see ya because you can't turn the ghetto into a Black Korea."

This musical description of struggle arose from real urban centers of increasing racial and economic strife. In South Central Los Angeles, numerous large plant shut downs contributed to a black male jobless rate of about 50 percent in some areas. The poverty rate

[1] Du Soon Ja was a Korean Liquor store owner on trial for the murder of a young black girl, Latasha Harlins, who was found shot in the back with the money for her purchase in her hand.

of Asians in LA County grew to twice that of whites. The poverty rates for Blacks and Latinos grew past three times that of whites. At the same time, the succession of Korean immigrants into small business in the South Central Los Angeles area created a new ethnic petit bourgeoisie or a "middleman minority." The convergence of these factors set the context for new conflicts and tensions between the people of Los Angeles. This conflict was only beginning to peak at the start of the 1990s.

"The oppressed should rebel, and they will continue to rebel and raise disturbance until their civil rights are fully restored to them and all partial distinctions, exclusions and incapacitations are removed."
—Thomas Jefferson, Notes on Religion, 1776. Papers 1:548

The violent reality of these as well as other social tensions awoke in the night on April 29, 1992. After four Los Angeles police officers were found not guilty of brutality against Rodney King, rage exploded in Los Angeles. 623 documented fires lit up the skies. Sixty people were killed and over two thousand people were counted as injured. The estimated damage was one billion dollars. Between April 29 and May 5, 1992, 12,545 people were arrested. 51 percent of those arraigned were Latino, while 36 percent were black.

Much of the initial commentary by the news media described the rioters as not human or as criminals. The rioters were often called savages. They were described as "going crazy." As many of the musicians I interviewed explained, the rioters were not wild animals but family members, friends, and neighbors. The newscasters were not explaining the reasons why this was happening. Few asked important questions about who was involved and what their emotions and motives for action were.

In contrast, Reverend Cecil L. Murray was a voice of clarity. While speaking at the First AME Church during the riots, "We did set some of those fires, but we didn't start any of those fires. Those fires were started when some men of influence decided that this nation can indeed exist half-slave and half-free."

One of the founders of Ozomatli, Will-Dog Abers was nineteen years old and lived near MacArthur Park during the Uprising. Will-Dog also saw the need to look back into history to identify motives and contributing factors in any attempt to understand what happened and why. A few years after the Uprising, Will-Dog worked on a production of a play with inner-city kids called Resistance 502 (in reference to five hundred years of resistance, since Columbus). He worked with the kids to research the motivations for the Uprising. They came to the conclusion that the Uprising was not caused by a couple of isolated events, but rather a long history of oppression. Will-Dog explained, "You have to go back into history, to Columbus, to slavery, to immigrants, to understand why this happened."

In addition to the dehumanizing, sensationalistic commentary by the news media of the rioters, there was a notion that everyone was out to get white people. It seemed like a tactic to scare people into racializing themselves—to band together racially for protection. As Quetzal Flores of the band Quetzal reflected in February 2002: "The media played it out like it was everyone versus white. Not everyone went out and said kill whitey. I think people were honestly thinking that this system is f*cked up and is racist. There are a lot of poor people and the majority of these poor people in Los Angeles happen to be non-white. It is important to have a class, race, gender analysis. But even that is not always enough to draw conclusions about why people do what they do. Basically, it was putting people's back against the wall and then giving them the reason to react, to explode. Rodney King was the reason. That was it. I know a lot of Mexicans who hate black people, and they were looting. Not because they were pissed off about Rodney King, but because it was time to get theirs, and their baby needed diapers, or they needed a carton of eggs and milk."

Contrary to certain stereotypes, thousands of people did not wake up that morning and say, *Today, I am going to loot, set things on fire, and kill whitey.* The Uprising was an emotional and political response to oppression. People had been beaten down, dehumanized, and now they were fighting back. And they were fighting back by destroying things.

As will.i.am, a member of the hip hop group the Black Eyed Peas (who was sixteen years old and lived in East LA during the Uprising), explained, "If you get angry, let's say your girlfriend broke up with you, you are going to kick the nearest thing to you. You're not going to go down the block and sock somebody else's shit."

Many of the first TV news journalists reporting live on the Uprising made quick analogies to the 1965 Watts Riots along the lines of: Thirty years later, America is still two societies—one black and one white. As they spoke, the picture behind them on the television showed neither black nor white people.

Most commentaries and publications on the '92 Uprisings have operated with images of American cities etched into our minds during the post-World War II era. These are comfortable images because they suggest a simple understanding of the events: the ghettoization of African-Americans, the suburbanization of the white middle class, racism, and police brutality. These are the terms we carry in our tool bag from the previous round of urban Uprisings in the 1960s. These terms were readily available and seemed to fit here and there in the analysis of the 1992 Uprising, but they ultimately fog our view of the reality of contemporary Los Angeles.

Literal black and white thinking is not sufficient for the interpretation of what happened. The Long Beach-based band Sublime made this point in their song "April 29, 1992":

"Cause everyone in the hood has had it up to here, it's getting harder and harder each and every year. I saw a baby go inside with her mother. I saw when they were leaving they were holding some Pampers. They said it was for the black man, the Mexican, and not for the white man. But if you looked in the streets it wasn't about Rodney King. It's about this f*cked up situation and these f*cked up police. It's about coming up and staying on top and screaming 187 on a motherf*ckin cop. It's not in the paper it's on the wall. National Guard. Smoke from all around."—Sublime

The Uprising was a moment of reckoning for many LA musicians. Benny Cassette, an artist/producer on the record label Island Def Jam, was fifteen years old during the Uprising and lived in the Silver Lake section of LA, where looting was taking place just a few blocks away. Benny described how he had do make a decision whether he would join some of his friends and loot local stores or stay inside his home. While he understood why many of his friends were looting, he decided not to take part. That decision was a personal turning point for him that became a larger question of faith and his purpose in life and soon after he started his spiritual journey as a Ba'hai.

Sitting with him in February 2002, he talked about that decision during the Uprising, and how that moment affects him and his music today. He said: "The riots made me feel like I had a purpose. It made me feel that I had a responsibility, and it inspired me to take that responsibility upon myself and try to do something with my arts."

As an artist in post-Uprising LA, he is aware of his role his community in addition to his personal success as musician. And he does not work in isolation. He has absorbed a wide range of influences from hip hop to soul to rock, which had often been segregated genres when he was growing up. For example, one of the songs he is working on for his new record is a collaboration with the country music artist Willie Nelson and the hip hop artist Mos Def.

Will-Dog Abers also considered the Uprising to be a defining moment in his life. He stated that, "At the time I wasn't really doing anything. Nothing really mattered to me. The Uprising was a major turning point for me. I realized that I needed to do something positive." In the years immediately following the Uprising, Will-Dog became involved in local community organizations such as the Los Angeles Conservation Corp, attempted to start a union, and helped form the group Ozomatli to raise money for the Peace and Justice Center.

This responsibility of seeing oneself as a member of the community with an active role in it, is shared by the Los Angeles band Quetzal. Quetzal Flores, who was eighteen years old at the time of the Uprising, grew up in the El Sereno section of Los Angeles and plays jarana, quatro, bajo sexto, and guitar with the band Quetzal. The musical influences of Quetzal span jazz, funk, R&B, jarocho (music of Vera Cruz), Cuban music, and various styles of Latin American music. When asked to describe the music of Quetzal he replied: "The music of Quetzal is a journey into the relationship between art and the responsibility of the artist to the community of struggle. Everything from the Chicano community to the gay community, any community in struggle."

Of course, not all musicians in Los Angeles share this view. Quazar plays keyboard and sings in the Frank Zappa-esque, Circus-like rock band Quazar and the Bamboozled. He also plays percussion with the Alice in Wonderland-like folk group Gwendolyn. Quazar was eighteen years old at the time of the Uprising and explained, "I was in a heavy metal band at the time of the riots, so it didn't really affect our music at all." And will.i.am of the Black Eyed Peas said that his musical movement was not political in nature but rather a personal movement to get his mother out of the projects of East Los Angeles.

But for LA bands such as Quetzal and Ozomatli, music started to reflect issues of struggle, though not a particular racialized struggle. The ethnic heritage of the band members of Quetzal spans Mexico, Central America, South America, Asia, and Europe. Quetzal is not just a Chicano band.

And the band Quetzal is not focused on one particular social issue. Quetzal Flores explained that they constantly have their antennas out listening and experiencing things that are going on out in the community. They make their "reports" in the form of songs. One of their songs is called "Cenzontle." Cenzontle is Spanish for mockingbird. The song is about a mockingbird flying through the valleys above Los Angeles that listens to the echoes in the valleys and repeats what it is hearing.

For the band Quetzal music is more than just an expression of emotion or even an expression of a political view. Music is a form of organizing. As Quetzal Flores explains, "I'm not just a musician, I am a community organizer. And I will organize through music because that's what I know how to do."

After the Uprising, many young LA musicians began to create an art and culture scene devoted not to making money through entertainment but the betterment of their community. Building this community of artists was a direct response to the riots. It was a direct response to the cries of the community. Troy Cafe, in the Little Tokyo section of Downtown, was the center of the scene in the beginning. But after Troy Cafe closed down in the mid-'90s, people continued to organize, and it has lasted until today.

This new outlook was also reflected in the music itself. Jose Espinoza grew up in East Los Angeles and was eighteen years old during the Uprising. He played saxophone with Ozomatli during the late 1990s. Jose explained that, "Before the riots, musicians were more about who they were and what neighborhood they came from. But after the riots a musical consciousness began to arise. People started writing about things they hadn't written about before. A diverse community of consciousness was formed."

"If that's not the future reality of the United States, there won't be any United States, because that's who we are."—Alice Walker when asked whether California, especially with its multiethnic society, represented the America of the twenty-first century [Reese Erlich, "Alice's Wonderland," an interview with Alice Walker, *San Francisco Examiner*, July 19, 1992, p. 12]

Los Angeles is an amazing compilation of varied cultures that reach out to every corner of the world and at the same time draw a wide array of influences into Los Angeles. This provides a rich testing ground for urban multiculturalism and what can be described as the new cultural politics of identity and difference, far removed from the imaginary melting pot of Anglofying Americanization. Reproduced on the streets and in its neighborhoods are microcosms of Taiwan, Vietnam, and Armenia. There is a Little Tokyo, a Koreatown, a huge long-established Mexican barrio, and a new barrio filled by a dense mix of Central American migrants representing Guatemala and El Salvador. The list of separate cultural worlds microcosmed in Los Angeles seems endless, but there is still another dimension to this complex panorama of urban multiculturalism, a cultural manifestation that may prove to be the most important new development arising from contemporary Los Angeles.

Multiculturalism is usually described first as the formation of segregated ethnic spaces (ghettos, barrios, Koreatown, Chinatown, etc.). Then there is a proliferation of conflict-ridden edges where different cultural worlds frequently collide in struggles to maintain cultural identity and cohesion. But something else is also happening in the urban borderlands of Los Angeles. Multiform "composite" cultures are slowly taking shape and being expressed on the local landscape and daily life—in the creation of new cuisines, designs, clothing, styles of popular art, and music; and in the development of new cultural and political identities.

Los Angeles, for example, has been a major center for the assertion of Latino identity (versus such government imposed categories as Hispanic or Spanish-speaking) as a means of uniting the diverse populations whose homelands stretch from Cape Horn to the Rio Grande. Many other forms of cross-cultural fusion and coalition building are taking place in the schools and neighborhoods, in community organizations and housing projects, in local government and cultural festivals, in ways that we are only beginning to recognize and understand.

LA's music scene is one of the best examples of this cross-cultural fusion. For example, the LA group Ozomatli is a self-described polyglot Black-Chicano-Cuban-Japanese-Jewish-Filipino crew that is committed to social change and community-building through the party pleasures of musical collision. "Ozomatli" is Nahuatl for the Aztec god of dance. With almost no big business support in terms of finance or advertising, they sold over 100,000 copies of their first album, Ozomatli (Almo Sounds, 1998) and have toured extensively throughout the world. Ozomatli's songs contain a fluid mix of lyrics in English and Spanish, which is reflective of the varied languages of Los Angeles. The multi-lingual aspect of their music might scare away record companies, but it does not frighten local fans, many of whom speak more than one language themselves.

Ozomatli's second album, Embrace the Chaos, released in September 2001 by Interscope, is chapter two in their plot to let the world know that the future of urban America is already here: already singing, and already dancing salsa to a hip hop samba.

Many of the topics of the Ozomatli's songs are familiar topics of oppression, police brutality, empowerment. However, when Ice Cube talks about "we" he means Black Americans. When Ozomalti uses "we" it is actually much more difficult to determine. Since the group describes itself as a polyglot Black-Chicano-Cuban-Japanese-Jewish-Filipino crew, "we" could mean any or all of the above. As Will-Dog explained, " 'we' can mean a lot of things, and the meaning can change."

"We" is in the process of becoming. "We" is not restricted or seen solely on the basis of race. When I posed the question of who "we" are to Quetzal Flores, he stated: "We are talking about the artist community that has grown out of East Los Angeles but has spread across the city—this network of artists that are thinking consciously about the future of our communities and taking an active role in determining the future of their community."

I then asked him if "we" was racially based and he said: "The city is divided racially. It might start out in a place where there are racial borders. But we are crossing those borders. For example, Medusa, a black hip hop artist, calls Quetzal up and says come play with us at Fais Do-Do because we think what you are singing about is important. And the people that come to my shows need to hear what you are talking about. And it works vice versa. And you begin to build that way. What brings Medusa, Quetzal, and Ozomatli together is race. But going beyond the racial analysis, seeing the larger picture at hand."

Who "we" are is not fixed solely in racial terms. It is fluid and at times plural in nature. It's similar to the Census Bureau, which struggles every ten years to figure out how to count people, and has to change its methods of counting almost every time. While this represents obstacles for the Census Bureau in proving demographic tabulations, it also affects our own sense of self. The deeper significance of America's becoming a plural society is what it means to the national psyche, to individual's sense of themselves and their nation—their idea of what it means to be an American.

"Now people are trying to be more community based. The community is building itself up, helping themselves out."–Jose Espinoza, February 2002

After the series of Uprisings in the 1960s came the Kerner Commission, a special panel appointed by President Lyndon Johnson to study race relations after the Uprisings in the 1960s. The panel came to the conclusion that America was moving toward two societies: one black, one white, separate and unequal. Many people were asking why after so many successes of the Civil Rights Movement there were riots. President Johnson tried to explain this in a speech he made at made at Howard University in 1965:

"You do not take a person who, for years, has been hobbled by chains and liberate him, bring him up to the starting line of the race and then say 'you are free to compete with all the others,' and then justly believe that you have been completely fair."

This condescending paternalism radiates to this day. People of color are made to seem like they are passive and helpless and always in need. So for forty years progressive work has been based around needs assessments—evaluating a community by identifying deficiencies. The reaction to the Uprising by many young musicians was that this way of thinking does not work. We have been doing needs assessments for forty years and what have we gained?

Quetzal Flores explained: "We are not reactive with our music, we are proactive. We don't do needs assessments, we do assets assessments. We have done a tremendous job of organizing in terms of creating this art and culture movement that exists in East LA right now. The path is actually very simple. You have a group of bands. They all need support. So you support each other. You do fundraisers for each other, you record CDs and you move like that. Everyone has done it—Ozomatli, Atzlan Underground, Quinto Soul, the Blues Experiment. We have all played for each other's fundraisers and that in essence is a proactive approach. We are not waiting for something to happen. We are not waiting for record companies to hand us the big deals. We are taking our future into our own hands."

This shift of thinking is one of the most significant effects of the '92 Uprising. Thousands of grant proposals have been written in the City of Los Angeles with sections on needs assessments. In fact, almost all grant proposals are formatted with a section on needs assessments, and how the need will be met. While it can be very useful in distributing funding and creating programs, it also sends a message that there is something wrong with the community and people outside of the community are the only ones able to fix it. Neighborhoods in Los Angeles are vibrant communities full of assets, not deficits.

Our community bled during the 1992 Los Angeles Uprising. And it bled in an area not as spatially restricted as Watts. We bled from Pacoima to Pomona, from Pasadena to Hollywood, from San Pedro to South Central. And the bleeding was also not racialized.

123

The entire community bled. And a simple band-aid would not solve the problem. Nor would a president's promise of a Great Society. The Uprising forced us to fundamentally rethink the ways we look at the problems in our city and ourselves. George Gershwin, a 20th Century American composer, said that, "True music must repeat the thought and inspirations of the people and the time." And the music of Los Angeles has followed that course. A musical community of consciousness began using music as a tool for organizing. Music became a tool for the empowerment of our community. Community issues would be addressed from the bottom up. And while music alone is not the way to salvation for our communities, art is an important component of this progressive movement. Furthermore, music gives us insight into who we are. For as Ralph Waldo Emerson wrote, "Music takes us out of the actual and whispers to us dim secrets that startle our wonder as to who we are, and for what, whence, and whereto." So we should listen to what is coming out of Los Angeles. Because it is a glimpse into all of our futures:

"Are you a soldier who fights against fraud or pawns in this game on this government's chessboard? The signs are clearly defined it's really your mind state. War's coming my people so stay awake."
—Chali 2na (Ozomatli, 1998)

This essay was complied from interviews and discussions with (in alphabetical order):

Will-Dog Abers—Will-Dog was nineteen years old and lived near MacArthur Park in Los Angeles during the Uprising. He currently lives in Echo Park and plays bass with Ozomatli. Ozomatli's second album, Embrace the Chaos, was released in September 2001, and won a Grammy award for best Latin Rock/Alternative Album in 2002.

Anand Bennett—Anand was fifteen years old and lived in West Covina during the Uprising. He currently plays mandocello, bass, and piano with jazz groups throughout Los Angeles while inventing new instruments.

Benny Cassette—Benny was fifteen years old and lived in the Silver Lake section of Los Angeles during the Uprising. He is currently an artist/producer with Island Def Jam, and still lives in Silver Lake.

Jose Espinoza—Jose was eighteen years old and lived in East Los Angeles during the Uprising. He currently lives in Echo Park and plays saxophone and sings with his group Umbalaye.

Roberto Flores—Roberto is a long time community organizer in Los Angeles, and is Quetzal's father. During the Uprising, his car was stolen in South Central Los Angeles and then was returned freshly washed with not a single item missing.

Quetzal Flores—Quetzal was eighteen years old and was attending college in San Francisco at the time of the Uprising. He grew up in the El Sereno section of Los Angeles and currently lives in Highland Park. Quetzal plays jarana, quatro, bajo sexto, and guitar with the band Quetzal. Quetzal's second album, Sing the Real, was released in March 2002.

Amad Jackson—Amad was thirteen years old and lived in the Silver Lake section of Los Angeles during the Uprising. He is currently an actor in Los Angeles.

Joaquin Nabarrete—Joaquin was fifteen years old and lived in West Covina during the Uprising. He currently lives in Echo Park and plays guitar and sings with his group Joaquin.

Dante Pascuzzo—Dante was fifteen years old and lived in the Sun Valley section of Los Angeles during the Uprising. He currently lives in Echo Park and plays bass with Quetzal and Makina Loca. Quetzal's second album, Sing the Real, was released in March 2002.

will.i.am—will.i.am was sixteen years old and lived in East Los Angeles during the Uprising. He is currently working on the next Black Eyed Peas album.

Quazar—Quazar was eighteen years old and lived in the Sylmar section of Los Angeles during the Uprising. He currently lives in Silver Lake and plays piano and sings with his group Quazar and the Bamboozled and plays percussion with Gwendolyn.

126

DESTRUCTIVE ENGAGEMENT

Gary D. Phillips

A South African friend of mine was visiting Los Angeles a week before the city immolated on the fires of neglect and rage. He'd lived here while attending the then Graduate School of Urban Planning at UCLA, and had returned to Johannesburg to head the urban policy section of the Urban Foundation—a liberal-to-left think tank plotting economic strategies and tactics for a new South Africa.

Over some Cuban food and a few beers we kicked it as to how in the fifteen months since he'd last seen LA, the city seemed to be fraying more. Not from the edges, but from the center outwards. He also reflected that JoBurg was not so different than the city of lost angels: Whites ensconced behind high walls shrouded in webs of electronic security, a growing chasm between those who want and can get and those who go wanting, an exploited immigrant labor force, and recession and crime at an all-time high.

Yet like the promise of a shiny mansion on a distant hill, the allure of a coming economic boom seduces both cities: JoBurg positioning itself to become one of the centers of finance capital which will infuse the whole of southern Africa; and Los Angeles waiting to reap the rewards as the center of Pacific Rim finance. The city is building huge skyscrapers and massive office complexes on spec—allowing for numerous vacancies against future returns—while in some areas of town African-American and Latino males suffer double-digit unemployment.

We talked of those economic matters, films we'd seen, books we wanted to write, and of course the pending verdict in the trial of the four cops who beat Rodney King. My friend, who is white, left Los Angeles a day before The Verdict and the whirlwind it unleashed. He and I made commitments to keep in touch as the uncertainties of our respective hometowns played themselves out.

Wednesday afternoon, the 29th of April, all of LA, and certainly other parts of the country, awaited the jury's decision in the courtroom located in east Ventura County. In particular this was the bucolic Simi Valley, site of the Ronald Reagan Library.

I hadn't been that anxious about a news report since I was in high school and couldn't concentrate on homework and kept turning on the TV to see who'd won the first Ali-Frazier fight. But this outcome would have a far greater impact than the arena in Madison Square Garden.

This arena of Simi, thirty-seven odd miles to the north and west of Los Angeles, was, and is, more than just another bedroom community begun by white flighters. It is a community, like Mission Hills, Manhattan Beach (Shaq, who lives there notwithstanding), or Newhall, where the cops, as civilians, interact with people in the super market, the bowling alley, and on front lawns. Not like the inner city where young black and Latino men more than likely deal with cops who prone them across the police cruiser on Martin Luther King, Jr. Boulevard.

And so a few minutes after three that afternoon, the radio played the measured tones of the sixty-five-year-old forewoman who said that the jury had found the four cops innocent of all criminal charges, save for a secondary count against Officer Lawrence M. Powell (the man who struck Rodney King the most times) for abuse under color of authority. The jury was hung only on this count. Post verdict, and in the wake of the massive reaction to it, the then LA District Attorney Gil Garcetti requested a retrial of Powell on this charge. But that afternoon, relatives and supporters of the cops celebrated in the courtroom while black folks throughout LA watched their televisions like Regis just pimp slapped a contestant for messing up on "Who Wants to Be a Millionaire."

Sitting in my office at that time of the Liberty Hill Foundation (a progressive funder of grassroots organizations in Santa Monica, California) I wondered abstractly if the work of reverend Cecil Murray, Congresswoman Maxine Waters, City Councilman Mark Ridley-Thomas, and others would go for naught. Since the previous Thursday, when the jury sequestered itself, these community leaders had been putting the word out that people had to be cool no matter what decision came down. There would be organized rallies and speakouts for the populace to vent their frustration. But the acquittal came a week and a half after an appellate court upheld the ruling of Judge Joyce Karlin in the Soon Ja Du case. Mrs. Du was a Korean storeowner convicted by a LA jury of second degree murder in the death of black teenager Latasha Harlins. Karlin gave Du five years probation rather than the sixteen years maximum in prison others had received under similar convictions. The judge said Mrs. Du going to jail wouldn't serve justice.

And so unanswered anger and blind fury collided at the intersections of Florence and Normandie in South Central. By dusk of the 29th, rioting and firebombing and looting had jumped off. Like Watts in '65 when I was a kid, you could watch the action on TV. Unlike Watts in '65, where shit was confined to a specific area, the anarchy spread from South Central to Koreatown, to Pico-Union, the edges of Silver Lake, Mid-City, and on into Compton, Long Beach, Pasadena, Inglewood, and even the gilded confines of Beverly Hills. Not only could you see it live and in color, but you were part of the action too.

Yet on Thursday morning we thought the worst might be over—psychologically tricking ourselves into thinking that one night's blowout would equal years of injustice. I went to work but my wife wisely decided to keep our, at the time, small children home from their preschool. Sure enough, Thursday afternoon the descent into the "riddle of violence" as African liberator Kenneth Kaunda phrased it, began again.

I rushed home midday from the office to find my neighborhood of Mid-City poised to go under the knife. The family gathered at a friend's second story duplex with others, feeling as though we were in a nameless land experiencing an ill-conceived coup. People were clamoring in the streets, darting here and there as gun shots whined through the air, cars slammed into each other and buildings, sirens screamed, and police and news helicopters swarmed about pyres of flame like giant mechanical moths. Shit was happening all around, the neighborhoods were a torrent of rip and run, yet all you could do was watch out your window—unsure of who was in charge and who wanted to be.

Stores not five blocks from us blazed red and grey into the darkening sky as the local Vons at Pico and Fairfax was looted. Three middle-aged women, one with a pistol in her apron pocket, stopped a roving band of gangbangers from torching the Texaco station at the corner of our friend's duplex on Ogden. When night arrived, my wife Gilda drove our children Miles and Chelsea out to another friend's house in Van Nuys in the Valley for relative safety. But being the proud petty bourgeoisie homeowner, I decided to stay at our crib so it wouldn't be empty.

So on a small table next to the live drama on my TV set rested my loaded Smith & Wesson .357 Magnum and a half-pint of courage-in-a bottle Jack Daniels—a volatile combination in the best of circumstances.

Well, the house didn't burn down nor did anybody, fortunately, try to bust a cap in my dome. But two personal things happened to me as a direct result of the civil unrest. It turned out our kids were incubating chicken pox because at the time it was going around their preschool and you're supposed to let them get it to develop the immunity. But at my then thirty-plus years I'd never had the disease and subsequently got it 'cause of that Thursday afternoon being cooped up with them in our friend's apartment. And my dad, Dikes, who was alive then and seventy-nine, had also never had chicken pox and subsequently got it from me (he was living with us but in Kansas City visiting relatives when the riot erupted). We were both miserable.

And that summer of '92, I started to write my second book, which would become the mystery novel Violent Spring. I'd already written a previously unpublished book with the main characters—donut shop-owning private eye Ivan Monk, Superior Court Judge Jill Kodama, retired LAPD cop Dexter Grant, et al—but knew using the backdrop of the siege and its aftermath as it shook out racially and politically would be a compelling story. Ten years later, I'm still writing about Monk's travails and other stuff. And Los Angeles is still the sexy beast you can't help but look in the eye now and then and write about.

132

I lived in one of those sleepy Los Angeles neighborhoods, with 1920s duplexes sandwiched between '70s apartment buildings, that was so unremarkable it was used for a movie to depict a generic '70s residential street. Our only claims to fame on Wooster Street, just north of Pico and east of Robertson, were a blues bar named Jack's Sugar Shack at the end of the block and a quasi-celebrity living across the street. It was a quiet Persian-Jewish neighborhood where it was hard to find a cup of coffee on Saturday morning if you didn't know where to go, with the Elat market and its smells of spice and meat, and the Haifa restaurant famous for its falafels and babganoush. I suppose the presence of the orthodox Jews out walking everyday in overcoats and yarmukles, earlocks flying, made our neighborhood a sort of target for part of the riots.

What made the riots so hard for me is that they happened while I was a hundred miles away, in Lake Arrowhead at a teaching retreat, and I saw the Woolworth and the building that is now a Pearl Arts Supply six blocks away from my home burning to the ground. At first, I figured the reports of rioting in LA were probably inflated, since the media has a way of doing that, but when the leaders of the retreat called off the Duck Dance, which was being planned to make me a better college instructor (I kid you not), I knew something was up. All of the teachers from our college who had been led away from the somber canceling of the Duck Dance huddled around the television watching in disbelief. Unlike my colleagues, who mainly lived in the suburbs surrounding Covina and Claremont, I lived only blocks from where the flames were going down. And, my husband and brother were in LA, closer to the violence than I could believe. A kind of weird calm overtakes me in a crisis, due to, I think, some early training from my alcoholic father, but with the telephone circuits busy and no way to call my loved ones in Los Angeles, I began to cry. It was strange to be so far from home, in a sort of twilight zone of poetry writing, hot tubbing, stick-on name tags, and big trees, watching violence spread over the LA basin.

When I got home the next afternoon in my Volkswagen laden with food and water a friend had told me to buy, the glare was tremendous and the streets seemed eerily deserted. I passed the local Vons on Fairfax and the National Guard was setting up their makeshift headquarters in the parking lot. The smell of smoke came into my house and hung there like a shroud for days. The ash fell like gray snow. And worst, the helicopters churned day and night—loud and low, making me afraid to leave the duplex. My husband Alan and I rented a video, something odd and sentimental like *The Thin Man Returns* or *Arsenic and Old Lace* and ate store-bought chocolate chip cookies. We were numb. It seemed strange to eat and sleep and do all the normal things with the smoke and tension hanging in the air.

I remember seeing Rodney King on television that weekend, too. That famous "can we all just get along" speech was something I heard, but it was his sweater that fascinated me. That sort of Mr. Roger's cardigan over his shirt and tie. Like someone else had dressed him and combed his hair and told him what to say. It was Sunday morning, I think, and it felt strange to be watching television with everyone else. I remember thinking it looked painful for Rodney King to talk and required more concentration for him to say those words than anything I'd ever done. As I watched him speak slowly and haltingly, I thought it would be a long time before anyone ever listened.

GUILTY AS CHARGED

Renée A. Ruiz

You ask me where I was those infamous days and nights of the LA Riots, and immediately, I want to lie. I want to shake my head slowly, lower my tone like I, in spite of everything, can't believe it ever happened and say, "Yeah, man. I was there. Saw it all firsthand. The things I could tell you. Crazy-mad. Crazy." Then, scratching the side of my head, I would quietly squint into the distance as if the fires were still burning and smoke was clouding my eyes. To make you believe, I would mumble something low, too incoherent for you to hear. I might swallow hard, as if about to cry.

After that, you wouldn't have to ask me. You'd know. You'd be thankful for my lies, for the woeful, danger-laced tale you could retell to outsiders of the experience, the ones with their noses pressed up against the glass, crowding each other out for a peek. Deep down, when the question came to mind, you knew the truth wouldn't do. You wanted my story. I wanted it, too.

Because truth is, if I hadn't had a television and lived in a LA County border town, I wouldn't have a thing to tell you worth hearing. Like everyone else who stomached the verdict on April 24, 1992, you would stand here before me, mouth agape in complete disgust at the lack of justice. "Where's the smoke? The shatter of glass?" Truth is, by circumstance I have been acquitted from any "real" riot experience. But I am guilty—guilty by association. Because I sat in the safety of my parent's apartment forty-five minutes from the epicenter, watched it all happen and didn't do a thing about it. Worse still, in some subconscious way I both sided with the rioters, wanted to be a part of the chaos, and yet criticized their seeming lack of forethought (why not loot the rich neighborhoods?), all the while ever glad to be, what then seemed to me at age seventeen, so far from it all. Yeah, I'm an accessory. The crime: standing idly by. Watching with a bag of popcorn in my lap, a frown on my face, and a gleam of jealousy in my eyes.

Certain specifics, like me being only seventeen and having the tunnel vision that comes with immaturity, the luxury of living in a predominantly white and middle-class town from which LA stood as a hazy glimmer in the distance, I cannot change. Nor can I hold myself accountable for the mistake my parents made in raising me to believe that good and evil possess colors. Terrifying moments as a child while kneeling before a pale, thin Christ during Mass still haunt me. Because no matter how bright and snow-white my dresses were, I wore my dark skin like sin. How I prayed that Almighty God was colorblind! Like taking my first communion, I swallowed this notion whole, thankful that my parents had set me straight. I knew who to play with, who to avoid, who to save, and who to blame. The very little Spanish I knew included ten derogatory names for various races. What a shock then, as a young adult, to repeatedly witness the exact opposite, to see with my own eyes whiteness equated to badness?

I know what you're thinking. My experience is not an isolated or unique one. There probably isn't a person I know who hasn't had to reprogram him or herself to stop fearing the Other, to realize that evil has no outer distinction from good. Bad people come in all colors. Simple. I suppose I had that figured out long before the Rodney King beating. But what continues to baffle me is that for all the centuries we as a people—united by land, longing, and circumstance—have spent getting over our own color issues, Justice lost her blindfold in a single day. So the riots began. And the whole state stood gaping in shock and disgust. What was the expectation? Were people supposed to shrug and walk off peaceably, with the hope that next time her blindfold would be tied tighter?

Even now, ten years later, I can't seem to pick out from among the line-up a suspect that matches the description of truth. I know it's stupid to run from the police and wrong for them to abuse their authority. These things, I then naively assumed, were common sense and I had no doubts that the jurors of the King case would agree. Like my mother had always told me, two wrongs don't make a right. Of course the four police officers involved would have to suffer the recourse for their use of unnecessary force. And of course, after he healed, Rodney King, too, would also have to pay for the crimes he committed that got him pulled over in the first place. These things, I—we—assumed were givens. The sun rises in the east and sets in the west. Anything tastes good deep-fried. If you do the crime, you should do the time.

But then the unexpected happened and instead of justice, the Los Angeles community was handed some matches and a tanker full of gasoline. The rest, as they say, is history.

That my memories of that moment in time derive from television, reality's worst imitator, saddens me. Am I embarrassed by the implications of this disclosure? Hell no. For one, I couldn't be more thankful that, because of my circumstances, I had the luxury of watching from a distance. No one except the looters wanted to be a part of it. Let's all get honest. I am not alone, the sole criminal of voyeurism with a red V emblazoned upon my breast. We all watched. Some of us from our safe living rooms miles away, others from our living room windows, or from the street corners where the fires were burning the brightest. And we were all just as glad that, years later, we'd be able to glance back at the riots and exhale with ease. Every single person old enough to remember, let alone understand, the LA riots has an alibi.

Hollywood has refused to recreate the riots on television and the big screen. Some owe it to the big/small complex, the event being all-encompassing but too close to home to sustain objectivity. Some just want to forget anything ever happened and move on for fear that attention might stir up certain defenses. And yet I wonder, wasn't that the point? Even ten years later when I think back to the first night of the riots, one thing sticks out in my mind more than anything else. On TV against a background of scowling protesters (that's what the news reporter had called them then, protesters) one man rushed into the camera's scope and shouted, "Crime against humanity!" And wasn't it though? Four white police officers walk after practically the whole world watched them (repeatedly, thanks to the news media) beat senseless a cowering, unarmed black man. How could people not get defensive? This country was founded on Christian theology, not Buddhist. Americans don't ever walk away from someone who pushes them. They punch back. An eye for an eye. And then some.

Now I'm not getting patriotic. Righteousness is the farthest notion from my mind. And I don't believe that looting grocery and furniture stores in your own neighborhood, then burning them down all in the name of justice is too bright an idea. Neither do I see the justice in dragging an innocent truck driver from his cab, cracking him over the head with a brick, and kicking the shit out of him. More than half of what I—we—watched happened on our TVs, through our windows, and opposite those street corners, happened not in the name of justice but in malice. Yet we cried, someone has to pay! Can't let them get away with it! This is Los Angeles, damn it, not some backwoods, ass-backwards, one-cow town in the Deep South! We're modern! Liberal! In need of free stuff! Someone has to pay!

And pay we did.

It has been nine years since my last visit to LA proper. February 1993 I was eighteen, living on my own, and almost too eager to see if, finally, TV and reality meshed. Deciding to "play it safe," I headed on the 91 freeway mid-morning in my low-profile, silver Geo Metro. On the passenger seat, beside a fresh pack of Marlboro Lights, sprawled a city map with all the "affected" areas highlighted in bright pink. I had even packed a lunch of white rice, ramen noodles, and a Diet Coke. Only two things distinguished me from one of those cheesy Hollywood tours: a guide and a PA system.

As I expected, the scars were still there. Bare, exterior walls jutting up like the bleached bones of what once were new businesses built on the promise of rehabilitation. Every street mourned the gutted remains of buildings destroyed by arson fires. Vermont. Western. Crenshaw. All these places I remembered from TV, news cams, and aerial shots. Minus the milling and violent crowds, it almost seemed to still be happening. Suddenly, as I stopped at the intersection of Manchester and Crenshaw, I got this creepy feeling. Visions of innocent people being dragged out of their cars, their cars being turned over and burned rushed into my head. Did one of those thugs on the corner just look at me? I began to smell smoke and scanned the block for any telltale, white plume. I couldn't breathe. What was I thinking, driving into the heart of darkness? My hands, now clammy, tried fruitlessly to cling onto the steering wheel. In my head that voice (my mother's, no doubt) was shouting now: Get the hell out! The car behind me backfired. Thinking it was a sniper I screamed only to look up and see that the light had turned from red to green.

So call me a coward. I'll be the first to agree. I couldn't even stomach revisiting the scene of the LA riots, let alone claim some right to the experience. As expected this confession will bring some level of censure my way. This is not what you came to hear, paid to see, or wanted to remember. But I realized one thing before the first word was written: I have no story to tell. As for my recollection of the LA riots, nothing exists but some scattered memories of news clips, "live" footage, and some other informational tidbits anyone could look up on-line. And a big part of me is deeply saddened by this fact. We were all there but didn't really see a thing. Like blindfolded witnesses to a collision, only aware that something happened but regrettably, confusedly still asking where, how, and above all, why?

HIDING FROM THE LA RIOTS

Greg Sarris

I had a plane to catch. 7:15 p.m., LAX to San Francisco. Eleven o'clock the next morning I was scheduled to give a keynote address at Foothill College, forty minutes from the San Francisco airport. I was a first-year assistant professor at UCLA, and a keynote address would be a good line on the resume. The topic of my talk: multicultural education at the end of the century.

The day before, sometime in the afternoon, while I was teaching "Introduction to American Indian Literature," the verdict was handed down: all police officers innocent in the beating of Rodney King. Driving home, I heard the first reports of rioting. Eleven o'clock that night, I watched the news coverage: images of people running in the streets, looting, breaking glass, black- and brown-skinned people; a truck driver beaten outside his truck at an intersection.

I was oddly unmoved. Not that I wasn't angered by the verdict. Rather, I told myself that if the police didn't quell the rioting then it would die of its own volition, or, more precisely, its lack of volition. One of my rants, as a person who came of age in the late '60s, was that people didn't care enough to exert themselves over political and social issues. And, if by chance they did exert themselves, who would listen? Who would watch the parade?

The next morning, I saw the smoke from my front-room window. I rented a small apartment, the upper portion of a house, actually, in the hills just above Hollywood, and from the front room I had a south-easterly view of downtown Los Angeles, which, on clear days, looked like a faraway and magical city on a hill. But now a portion of that city was blocked, the skyscrapers hidden behind dark clouds that wreathed ever so slowly, lifting as if from a violent aperture in the earth's surface. Shaving, I listened to the news: the rioting was spreading—the word the radio host used. Still, I wasn't particularly interested or concerned. Oh, I suppose I hoped the rioting would continue. But, for all my anger over the verdict, it seems in retrospect that I wanted the rioting to continue if only to prove that people still cared.

I went about my business. Graded papers. The gym. Began preparing my keynote address. In that apartment, I always worked at my dining room table, where I could see the view, a portion of it anyway, from behind my stacks of paper and books. As I wrote lines such as "sensitivity to difference" and "a concern for what we don't know must predicate any pedagogy we embrace," a familiar anxiety arose in me and with it the same question: Who was I to speak? Specifically, who was I to speak as an authority on issues of multiculturalism?

I am fair skinned. My eyes are blue. My mother was white, a German Jew, to be exact. Never mind that my father was American Indian (Coast Miwok) and Filipino—I never knew him. I was adopted and raised by middle-class white people; yes, until the age of nine or ten, my so-called formative years, until my adopted father sent me off, or back. So, as a speaker on issues of multiculturalism, wasn't I just posturing? Worse, wasn't I using a part of my blood heritage—the American Indian part—for my own gain? What did I know of the multicultural experience? When would I be found out?

The questions had come up so frequently and for so long in my experience that by now they presented themselves plainly as a knot in my stomach. I felt anxiety, and then the fear, the urge to protect myself and hide. And then, the fighting back, the answers, the parts of my life that might arm me, make me legitimate, translate "safe," once again. After the age of nine or ten, my life with Indian and Mexican people, many of the Indian people my relatives, even if I didn't understand the connection then. And, I know my Indian culture and history. And my father, even if I didn't know him, was Indian, dark-skinned. And my aunt, his sister, says she can look at me and see I'm "not all Caucasian." My God, and I've been elected tribal chairman. The Indians—my people—recognize me as Indian. My hair gets darker, thicker, and straighter. My light skin shows a hint of olive. My eyes turn brown.

A tentative peace, a momentary calm, and I was able to finish the notes for my address. I packed and made reservations for a 4:30 cab, gave myself plenty of time to get to the airport, given LA's rush-hour traffic. When the cab had not arrived at 4:45, I called the dispatcher, a woman who told me "the driver was in a jam but on his way." Outside my window, I saw the wreathing black smoke had traveled west. It lifted in enormous gusts, as it had earlier, but it seemed darker now, blacker; and the gusts rose faster, more urgently, twirling into the air and moving as if the chasm from which it was spewing was widening. For the first time, the smoke was close enough so that I could see it was traveling in my direction on Hollywood Boulevard, which was only a half mile below my home. Newscasters verified what I could see: the riot was out of control and moving closer to me.

5:15, still no cab. I called the dispatcher again. No answer this time. Suddenly, it occurred to me that I might not make my plane. At six o'clock, I learned the alarming truth from the dispatcher of another cab company: no cabs were running.

By that time, the smoke was directly below me, a vertical line from me to the boulevard. And something more: neighbors were constructing a barricade with trash cans at the bottom of the hill, sealing off our street. One man behind the barricade held a rifle. I was trapped. I wasn't getting out. What if the rioters moved off the boulevard and into the neighborhoods, as they were threatening?

I called friends, family. Stay or flee? But I couldn't flee, even if I could get my car past the neighbors' barricade. A curfew had been imposed. I would be stopped by the police. I panicked. Fear rose up.

It grew and enveloped me. I curled into a ball on the floor below my window, hands over my head, and vomited.

There is not a precise language you can give to moments like these, not while you are in the midst of them. Later, time and distance—and safety—allow you the opportunity to discern meaning, relevancy, to see the long line of the moment.

As I write about my experience of the LA riot now, ten years later, higher in the hills and purportedly safer, I recall another time in my life. Ninth grade and I was at a dance in a Vet's hall. The late '60s. What are you in ninth grade, fourteen? Most of the people at the dance were older, juniors or seniors, or out of school altogether. My friend Mitchell Martinez and I were more or less tag-alongs, hangers-on with the older crowd. Anyway, at this particular dance, an Indian guy and a white guy started fighting, fists, torn shirts, the whole thing. A security guard broke them up, but by the time the band played its last number, everyone had heard what was going to happen outside after the dance—a rumble.

Indians and Mexicans lined up against whites in the parking lot. I saw chains, brass knuckles. Security guards were frantically attempting to radio the police. I recognized two of Mitchell's brothers, older Mexican guys to be reckoned with, in one line. They would know me. But would most of the others in that line? In the other line, the line of white guys, I saw the red-headed junior who'd called me "a white beaner" two weeks before in the third hall. I turned to Mitchell and told him that I thought we were too small to do any good. We split, tore through back alleys until we came up behind the corner grocery at the edge of South Park. Mitchell never saw me stop. He kept running, no doubt to his house a few blocks into South Park, where his family lived, like most Indian and Mexican families in Santa Rosa then. I crawled into an abandoned car behind the grocery, listening to the sirens, and only came out after the bread truck pulled up to the grocery first thing in the morning.

The long line of the moment. From that night of the LA riot to the night of the rumble; back and forth, and all the points in between. Like the times I'm with Indian relatives only to see the humiliation they experience when the waiter or salesperson talks to me first; or the humiliation I feel when one of them unwittingly says to me, "Your father's downfall was white women." Or when white relatives ask what kind of food I eat or if I'm "into nature." When I have to prepare a lecture on multiculturalism.

In these moments, I am positioned by others on one side of the racial divide or the other. Sometimes I can choose. But whether I am positioned by others or am given the space to choose for myself, I must land on one side or the other. There is not in reality at this time in America a borderlands home for me, for the stark reality is that, even if I create some ideal borderlands space, I will find myself on one side or the other, and in the more pronounced moments, like my experience of the LA riot and the rumble outside the dance hall, there will be danger wherever I land. With both the riot and the rumble, I felt I belonged with the non-whites, but would I be seen beyond my appearance? Would my feelings be seen and understood despite my exterior? Would my history, or at least a part of it, shine through? On the other hand, wouldn't the whites—the guy who called me "a white beaner," or the riot police—eventually see in me the enemy?

In Invisible Man, Ralph Ellison's nameless narrator says, "I am invisible, understand, simply because people refuse to see me." What he was saying was that, as a black man, white Americans refused to see beyond the color of his skin. That was in 1952. Forty-three years later, at the time of the LA riot, little had changed, albeit we had become more aware of race and race relations. Sure, in many places laws were changed, but in too few places could the same be said of attitudes. And, in the end, don't we still read one another by color? Aren't our readings always blind to some extent? I'm not suggesting that we should, or, contrary to Cinderella notions of certain liberals, that it's possible, to ignore color. We cannot escape the fact that as an American people we are tied to a history that is violent and racist in very particular—and changing—ways. But how do we read the racially mixed person, the increasing numbers of individuals with mixed histories who march in our direction?

If, for me, the moment of the LA riot stretches a considerable distance, then it also goes deeper. It's about a nagging sense of illegitimacy, the inner battles, the psychic violence of denial, the denial that coils in your stomach, so that no matter how often, or in what ways, you explode, nothing changes the fact that in some regard you are still homeless. Perhaps I should ask what the color of fear is.

The answers probably do have something to do with "sensitivity to difference" and that "a concern for what we don't know must predicate any pedagogy we embrace." And, certainly, the lived lives of those of us who are mixed can shed light on the country's multicultural history as it continues to unravel. But I know for sure the answers won't be easily seen or understood.

That night, after cleaning up the mess I made below my front-room window, I went to bed. Not to sleep, but to wait out the night. At some point, I dozed. I woke to silence, the absence of sirens. It was five-thirty in the morning. I called a cab, and yes, someone could pick me up in twenty minutes and drive me to the airport.

Tiptoeing, I found my Kipling knapsack and headed for the door. The town was empty. On La Brea southward, just below Baldwin Hills, a shopping center had burned to the ground, cinders smoldering in what now looked like an endless charred field. This is what it must look like to have been in a war, I thought to myself. The sun had not come up over the hills yet. A long shadow covered the land in every direction, as far as I could see. I knew I'd catch a flight.

LOOTING AND ENTERPRISE

Cristián A. Sierra

Either the telephone lines had been knocked out or they were so inundated with calls that the most they could produce was a sad clicking sound before the line went dead. I paced around the dorm hallway and tried to call again and again there was silence on the other end. No ring. Nothing. I paced the halls and everyone was in a daze. I felt helpless and sick inside. I called again. This time there was a recording: *All circuits are busy. If you wish to make this call, please hang up and try again.*

"They're starting fires," someone said.

I walked over and saw the images of Los Angeles burning on the TV. A helicopter camera paned the sprawling expanse of the LA skyline. Plumes of black smoke rose into the sky. Then the image switched to windows being shattered. Old and young people were strolling and running about with stereo equipment, groceries, and furniture.

"Why are they doing that?" someone said. "They're destroying their own neighborhood."

"It's like some sort of temper tantrum," someone else said.

"They aren't even Black. You see there. Those are Hispanics… I mean Latinos." Then someone else corrected, "Chicanos."

I didn't say anything. After my first year of college and a Chicano studies class I didn't know what the hell I was. But I felt pride welling up inside me. "My people are looting in solidarity with the Blacks," I said to myself. "Yes. What has the power structure offered us but cheap alcohol and expensive produce? You can't even find tomatoes for less than a dollar a pound in the ghetto. Fuck them."

Then there was an image of a liquor store being lit on fire. You could see a young man casually dowsing the flames with lighter fluid as if he were preparing for a barbecue, and the sick feeling came over me again. I went back to my room to call Bill. After calling over and over and not getting through, my persistence paid off and his sister picked up the phone.

"Are you OK?! Is the liquor store OK?!"

"Yeah we're OK. My dad sent Billy down to the store to make sure nothing happened."

"What! He'll be…" I stopped myself. "I'll call back."

I persevered at trying to get through to my mother and finally got through to her as well. The process was a mind numbing exercise in dialing, hanging up, redialing, and hanging up again and again.

Twenty minutes later my mother picked up. "I need to go to the market and pick up some milk," she said annoyed.

"No. You are not going."

"I think it will be okay," and as she said this I could hear sirens in the background.

"Don't go anywhere."

"Really Cristián," with a correctional maternal tone, "it's like a fortress here."

"And what is it like down the hill where the market is?"

"Well there are a few fires but I think I'll be OK."

The thought of my mother driving around in her light, rainforest green Infinity sedan, looking for an open supermarket with nonfat milk entered my mind and I was positively frightened.

"There are police everywhere," she added as if I should find the fact comforting.

"There are reasons for that."

My mother gave a heavy sigh. She lived on a hill between El Sereno and Highland Park in the northern part of East LA. The hill consisted of condominiums. Daryl Gates, Chief of Police of the Los Angeles Police Department lived here. He was seen by many as being responsible for the Rodney King beating and the LAPD's systematic harassment of minorities. The police my mother talked about were guarding him.

"No," I said trying to sound as forceful as I could without pissing her off, "stay inside."

"Have you called the Kims," she said changing the subject.

"Yeah. They sent Billy to the liquor store."

"Are they going to open today?"

Were the people of Los Angeles crazy? Images of lootings, beatings, shootings, and arson were playing over the television. Black smoke was rising into the hazy air. Sirens cried in the background and National Guard troops were on the way. Los Angeles was a war zone and Angelinos like my mother wanted to go on as if it were business as usual.

I pleaded with her not to leave the house until she relented and promised she wouldn't but added, "I don't know what I'm going to have for dinner then."

It was evening before I was able to get hold of Bill.

"They took everything," he said. "When I got there Hector was there convincing people not to break in but when they saw me the crowd forced me to open the doors." Hector was a local and worked at the store.

"At least you're OK," I said.

"Our customers just took everything they wanted. Some of them were just walking around with guns and I just kept saying 'go ahead, go ahead.'"

"God that's horrible. At least you're OK. You're really lucky."

"One after another they took everything…If my Dad hadn't made me go down there Hector would have been able to keep them from breaking into the store. The store was fine until I got there."

"Are you OK?" I asked.

"Some of them made jokes and tried to talk to me like regular. But all the while they were fucking us."

"Yeah," I said trying to console him, but he sounded completely numb. There was no emotion in his voice. "I'm glad you're OK. That's the most important part." But what the hell did I know what the important part was?

In the following weeks the Kims opened their store again and those same customers that had robbed them came back to buy their groceries. The fact that they had stolen from them would never be mentioned, but I wondered if something was lost between the Kims and their customers or if I was just being naïve and there was never anything there to begin with. The riots were a lot of things I'm sure, but one of the things it did was give seemingly good people license to think of themselves first and disregard their neighbor. Maybe it was because they themselves felt disregarded by the verdict or the power structure or whatever, but in many ways it was a sort of celebration—and lootings and fires were part of the festivities.

THE UNREST

T.E. Spence

My old man meant business all right. He was in his study, and he had his Korean War arsenal out on the desk and ready for action. He had on work boots and a dark brown jump suit. He had all of his legal files and papers cleared off the desk and stacked and organized in a corner. He was squared-away.

"It's coming up Vermont," he said. "They burned that shopping center down at Vermont and Santa Monica today." It had been going on for days. Smoke plumes rising up all around the city, branching out at the tops like palm trees. Ashes all over everything.

"Any action at your place?" he asked.

"A little." In fact, it had been an unusual afternoon in the neighborhood. I had gone out the back door to get my laundry, and then stopped and spent half an hour watching young men down on the Boulevard smashing store windows and grabbing bunches of stuff that they carried back to an apartment building a block away. Some guy in a sports car pulled over and yelled at them to stop what they were doing, and some of them did stop, but only long enough to throw what looked like large stones onto the guy's car. Whatever they were throwing made one hell of a racket against the metal and glass of the guy's car, and he took off in a big hurry.

"We sent you kids back to your Uncle Fuzzy's in '65. I stayed with the house."

I didn't remember that. My sister and I were little ones then. But it didn't surprise me much. Our house in View Park wasn't really close to the burning in Watts, but there had been as much fear and anger in the air over the city as there was smoke. Someone in the neighborhood had spray-painted something hateful that I didn't yet understand onto my mother's car, and my old man had driven the car around Los Angeles, uncovered, for a month.

But none of that bothered us kids. It was adult stuff. And anyway, we were back with Uncle Fuzzy on his little ranch outside El Paso, eating homemade peach ice cream and playing with horny toads.

"I had my Korea gear, and this," my old man said. He picked up a big pump shotgun. "Hard to miss 'em with this." The stock was burled brown wood. The contrast with the black metal of the barrel was almost beautiful, if you didn't think too much about what the thing was made for.

"I think you're set," I said.

He was wiping fingerprints off the barrel. "I surely am. Any no-count stepping foot on this property will wish to God he hadn't."

And there it was. The West Texas drawl. We never heard it in the house, growing up. I only heard it when I was a little older, and only when we were with people from the South. Like Brother Joe Matthews, whose congregation my old man "lawyered" for. Sometimes it sounded like a put-on to me, but I never could be sure. There were moments when it did seem real. Like tonight.

"Koreans are tough hombres," he continued. "Some people are going to find out about that."

He was talking about the Korean merchants patrolling their rooftops. You could be stopped at a light on your way down Vermont or Western and see reflections of faces and barrels of semiautomatic weapons in the window of the car next to you.

"I got some beans and cornbread downstairs, if you're hungry," he said.

"I think I'll head on back now."

"Suit yourself. I hope you're taking this thing seriously, T," he said.

"I am," I said.

"You still got that little .38, or do you need a pistola?"

"I got it," I said, and took off.

So, tonight I wouldn't be alone. There would be other men in small rooms all over the city, sitting up with me. Checking and loading weapons, then sitting and waiting with them, in the dark. I could tell them all about it. All except what they should be looking out for.

My old man was born onto the dirt floor of the Great Depression. Then he grew up and hopped a westbound freight headed somewhere else and never looked back until he got there. "Big City Lawyer," his people called him. He had defined his life, and knew its boundaries. If he had ever worried about what he was not, I never heard about it.

If not for him, and for the G.I. Bill and the Postwar Boom, I surely would be just another poor cracker boy working on the Santa Fe Railroad back in Amarillo. So it was, as he would say, just a cryin' shame that we never could talk. That it always felt like some rote pitch you just couldn't get over fast enough.

Because things were different with me. I never had much of what my old man called "direction." Not that I was stupid or lazy. Or lacked imagination. It was just that

I didn't care. I wanted to, or tried to want to, but just couldn't seem to. Couldn't seem to make myself. Care. Because to care you had to believe or not, and trying either was like lying to myself and then hoping to forget the lie. I did try, but I never could forget.

There were no cars on Los Feliz Boulevard, and the street lights were out, so it was quiet and dark, overhung by cool shadows of large trees. I breathed in night-blooming jasmine blowing onto my face through the window.

I cruised down Vermont and then swung east on Sunset, to Lemoyne in Echo Park. Good ol' 1316: Vintage 1920s. "Handy

Location." "Furnished" bachelor units, only $350 a month, utilities included. No pool, no pets. No smoking in bed. Last stop of broken-down Anglo-Saxon and Mexican-American men on small naval and railroad pensions. First stop of poor immigrant families from Guatemala and El Salvador. Have a nice day.

I pulled up to the curb. Clear. Quiet. No out-of-control burning, passions dancing up inside of people, making them itch and burn and run around screaming and breaking and taking things. They were quiet now. Burned out for now.

Only faint smoke smells and a little floating ash left over from the afternoon.

The rent was due. Was there time to pay Vern tonight? I checked my watch. There was still time. Time to pay Vern. And time to stand in the foyer and look at myself in the broken mirror. Time for Vern to open the door in worn slippers and greet me with weary determined heartiness. Time to see his obese, snoring woman in the flickering blue light of the midnight movie. Time to walk down the hall and hear Vern's pinched, petulant voice through the wall when she bothered him by asking who was that. Time to lie down in my room and breathe in the acrid high notes of the ashes left over from the fire in old man Sanchez's unit two years ago. Time to stare at the darkness and doze.

And time to wake up to the taxi driver next door with the Mexican woman that I never could get a good look at. Time for bed-springs and moaning and creeping down the hall and listening near a door. Time for creeping back to "my" place and flipping on the light and playing "catch-roach" with torn-off strips of fast-food napkins.

And time to take out my pistol and check it. And load it. And stand in front of the bathroom mirror and stare at it, and stare at me. And time to wonder: should I squeeze the universe into a ball and roll it toward some overwhelming question? Could I?

And time to say: "And why would I? I am neither poet nor prince, and here is no great matter."

And time to turn out the lights and open my pistol, and close it, and sit with it in the dark. And time to remember Aunt Dottie tucking me into bed and saying: "Pray to Jesus, Tommy. Jesus always hears you." And time to say: "One more night, Jesus. Just one more."

GEOGRAPHY OF RAGE

Jervey Tervalon

I don't think that Los Angeles much wants to remember the largest and costliest civil disturbance in the history of the United States. No, it's almost as though the city has some sort of amnesia, or maybe it's fear; fear that what happened then could jump up and bite us again.

For some the riot was almost a random event, linked tenuously to the Rodney King beating; another example of those damn black and brown folks getting out of hand again. At least that's what the media fed us. I guess their reasoning was that the minorities accepted police abuse before and didn't try to burn the city down, so why should 1992 be much different? This kind of reasoning is only viable when the natives are so far off you can't hear the drums pounding away, venting rage.

You see, Los Angeles is vast, vast and almost unknowable. What goes on in predominately Mexican-American East Los Angeles, is a world away from predominately black south central Los Angeles. And really, the Westside of Los Angeles is all there is for the predominately affluent white power brokers that run this city. I should have known better myself—sensed that the city was near conflagration—

that evening when the riot would start, mere miles from my Pasadena home. I would have been hunkering down with a shotgun and bottle of water and frozen food. Yet I decided to ignore the dire warnings and walk my dog.

My wife didn't want me to go, insisting that it was a stupid thing to do when television shows were being pre-empted by breaking footage of rioters setting ablaze palm trees in front of downtown's City Hall. I told her not to worry, that as a big man with a walking stick and a seventy-five pound Siberian Husky on leash, I felt fully capable of handling whatever might happen my way.

After crossing the street that was the major divide between my working-class neighborhood and the upscale one just a few blocks over, I was ready to enjoy another quiet stroll in the neighborhood above the Rose Bowl in Pasadena, California (Pasadena, that balmy city that hosts the Rose Parade every New Year's Day, is a scant thirteen miles from the epicenter of the coming unrest).

The protesters started downtown at Parker Center and seemed much like the Greens and other social activists protesting World Bank and IMF gatherings, but that was only the beginning; the riot rolled on, gathering in strength and viciousness—the National Guard who were called out to quell the disturbance had to wait forty-eight hours to be issued live ammunition—and by that time the riot had spread to dozens of neighborhoods. At first I shared that rage, that the police were totally out of control; that the city had earned its bitter harvest—but I didn't know then how intensely the fires were burning, or how sharp the odor of burned-out homes and looted businesses would be.

I turned onto Prospect Blvd., that lovely tree-lined street with the occasional mansion designed by Frank Lloyd Wright or the Greene Brothers. By the time I reached Arroyo Blvd., the street that overlooks the Rose Bowl, I heard the faint but unmistakable sound of staccato gunfire coming from around the Bowl. I heard it again, this time the sound of various caliber weapons and I was genuinely panicked. Looking into the darkness, I strained to see what was jumping off down below. Then tires squealed and I saw various cars roaring away from the Rose Bowl, up towards Prospect. I fantasized gunmen spotting me and thinking that I was a rich bastard that needed shooting.

What preceded Rodney King also reached the world in another black-and-white video recording. This time the camera caught the ugly confrontation between a black teenage girl by the name of Latasha Harlins, who was accused of stealing an orange juice from a corner market. Latasha Harlins hurled the orange juice at the shopkeeper and, for the world to see, on grainy videotape, the Korean shopkeeper shot Harlins in the head, killing her. The black community was enraged, but the shopkeeper was nonetheless sentenced to probation by a seemingly indifferent judge. People complained that if the shopkeeper had killed a dog in cold blood, she would have received a harsher sentence. They were probably right. Thus, for many of us, the videotape showing Rodney King being mercilessly beaten seemed to be cruel déja vu.

I trotted back to my working-class neighborhood, but not so quickly as to miss noticing how deserted the streets were. Just about home, I saw a black woman working on her car. I shouted to her that some fools at the Rose Bowl were shooting the place up. She sighed and shook her head. "I told those idiots not to be doing that. Nothing good is gonna come of shooting up the city. That's not gonna do nothing for nobody." I remember that woman's words more clearly than Rodney King's and the sound of gunshots reverberating in my ears on that cool Los Angeles night, and I wonder if they'll be another fire the next time.

JOBS WITH WAR

Andrew Tonkovich

First, where I am nearly ten years earlier, in October, 1983: A "day room," downtown jail, full of sweaty men in jumpsuits. The television, perched up in a corner of our cement-floored, cement-tabled, cement-walled unit is controlled by the guards, a whimsical and sadistic bunch. Sheriffs in training are sent here for a yearlong apprenticeship, presumably in community relations.

I want to see the TV news but, ridiculous as it sounds, on top of everything, we cannot get them to change the fucking channel.

Twenty-three years old. It's my first arrest. I'm scared, but so tired I don't care that I'm (1) stuck in a room with capacity of maybe 25, easily filled to three times that, and (2) that I am temporarily lost in the prison system—both consequences of notorious overcrowding, for which the county will later be sued. We lie like old men on old mattresses. I want to see news coverage of our arrests early that morning, a hundred nonviolent anti-nuclear protesters blockading military and weapons industry offices on El Segundo Boulevard in opposition to Reagan's Euromissiles.

Eleven o'clock. Finally, they change the channel. Instead of protests, a breaking story about the shooting of a long-time local newsman, silver-haired, homespun, doddering Jerry Dunphy, shot outside a restaurant in an armed robbery attempt. Jerry Dunphy? Who'd rob him, I wonder? "From the desert to the sea, to all of Southern California," he always began. Robbing Jerry Dunphy is like robbing Hobo Kelly or your uncle: You could do it, but you could do a whole lot better. The next news story: the bombing deaths of nearly 300 Marines in Beirut. Our timing couldn't be worse.

I've seen my father a few days earlier, at a birthday party for Mom. Dad's taken me aside, mentioning he's heard something at Hughes. Employees should expect delays on Monday morning. Protesters. He hopes I won't be among them, hopes that I won't be out there where he works, that he'd be embarrassed.

I'm a smart-ass, twenty-three, angry. Mom's wrapped presents are stacked on the hi-fi. There's a banner Dad made on the computer, printed out in awkward dot-matrix type: Happy Birthday!

"Dad," I say, "you never asked me if I was embarrassed—about what you do."

To be fair, it's from Mom and Dad that I got my sense of community service, responsibility, and my moral sense. I've stacked chairs, served cookies, been an altar boy at our church in Lynwood. But now the church in Lynwood is dying out, its elderly, conservative Midwesterner parishioners passed away or moved away. Betrayed, the remaining translucent old whites won't share their sanctuary, their god with "the Blacks," as they call them, or "the Mexicans." Some Sundays more people stand in the choir loft than the sanctuary.

Their own kids have long since moved to Cerritos, or faraway Orange County. Their kids are, apparently, not embarrassing them.

On that April afternoon in 1992, I drive with a friend on the San Diego Freeway, trying to beat curfew, trying to get home. Two white UC Irvine grad students, me married to a Mexican-American and she the mother of two Black kids. Lower middle-class, public school educated, we grew up here and became political people, she a former social worker, me a former activist.

I want to shout this autobiographical information from the car as we make our frustratingly slow way north from Orange County to Venice. Instead, we nod and smile nervously at the other drivers, even as we pass the Seal Beach Naval Weapons Station, where the bombs are kept, the nuclear weapons whose presence the military "will neither confirm nor deny." Past Long Beach Airport, Watts, the South Bay, Inglewood, spotting tufts of smoke like a couple of park rangers scoping a forest.

Car windows are rolled up. Other drivers and passengers look straight ahead, as if we are parked at a big drive-in or taking an eye test, concentrating when the optometrist asks, "what is the smallest line you can read?"

In the days immediately following the riots, I do what lots of our political friends and neighbors do: go to a big warehouse a couple miles from the fires to bag free groceries. The size of an airplane hangar, the name of the place is, weirdly, Food 4 Less.

We are assembled into teams, bucket-brigade or assembly-line style, packing contributions of cheesy crackers, canned goods, and powdered milk. Nobody sees us in there, inside that hangar. It feels like we are hiding. Group leaders offer strict instructions about what goes in the grocery sacks. Some people, I notice, follow the rules exactly. Some people disobey: They pack too much.

Lynwood, California advertises itself at its entrance with a red, white, and blue Captain America shield: "The All-American City." I was born there in 1960. Watts, where the riots took place five years later, is a five minute drive away.

When African-Americans started moving to Lynwood, those whites at our church started calling Lynwood "the All-African City."

In the sixties and seventies, Dad put on his black shoes and his thin tie, glasses, and security badge and drove to North American Rockwell, once in Downey, where we lived and where I grew up. After each space voyage, my brother and I, along with hundreds of Rockwell employees and their kids, met the Apollo astronauts in the massive Rockwell parking lot, where the space capsules were built. Later, we met Soviet astronauts. They seemed pleased to see us, patting my little brother on his crew cut. Nobody mentioned war. Not the Cold one, or Vietnam, or Belfast, or the Middle East. The cosmonauts smiled, nodded, and autographed one and five dollar bills. I wondered how enemies on Earth could be friends in space.

I chalked it up to weightlessness.

I delivered newspapers to nurses and patients at Rancho Los Amigos, once the country's biggest and most famous polio mylitis and spinal cord injury clinic. It was practically across the street from our 1950s tract home community, on the other side of Imperial Highway, a fifty-mile-long road, impossible to avoid if you want to see the basin. Imperial was once the preferred route to LAX. After the first riots, neighbors warned my nervous mother not to stop at lights, to lock her car doors, to run a red light if a suspicious "Black" came near. Eventually, she gave up, driving the additional miles south on the Long Beach Freeway to the 405 north.

After school one day, I stumble onto 10,000-watt lights, movie cameras, reflectors, generators, and thick cables. Coming Home, with Jane Fonda and Jon Voight, filmed against the backdrop of the Spanish mission-style architecture of the county hospital. I ride my ten-speed behind a movie truck, a camera mounted in back. I don't understand what I've seen until years later, when I finally see the film. Till then the closest I've come to the war is wearing a so-called memory bracelet, made of cheap copper with the name of a POW-MIA "serviceman" engraved on it. My wrist turns green, the bracelet finally breaks. My soldier does come home—I see him on television, getting off a plane. He lives in South Gate. He's Mexican.

Family history: My wife's white mother was meant to be the next Shirley Temple, the one from Racine, Wisconsin you never heard of. Her Mexican dad was on a WWII troop transport with Gene Kelly. My own grandmother, a divorcée photo retoucher from Great Falls, imagined she'd find work in Hollywood. Dad marched in the Rose Parade, playing his tuba. My parents saw Elvis perform once, at the Dorothy Chandler Pavilion. For the record, they didn't think much of him. That's show biz.

During summer school for "mentally gifted minors," I read books out loud to Rancho kids who'd had a painful operation: a spinal fusion. I pushed a lot of wheelchairs. Once I crowded into the surgical theater and watched the procedure. Bright lights. An intercom. It was like a very, very slow movie.

Eventually, my folks find a new church in Downey. No Blacks, but plenty of Mexicans, with their own separate Sunday morning service in Spanish. Aunts, uncles, and cousins move to Orange County, where I myself will live one day. We ride the Disneyland monorail and Autopia while Watts burns the first time, then drive our cars back to newer suburbs, where it is possible to live in a world where quotation marks define other people ("the Blacks," "the Mexicans"), but not, it seems, us.

Spring, 1984. Rodney King is about eighteen, Jerry Dunphy is probably back in the news saddle, the murdered Marines buried. Hobo Kelly was, by the way, a local television clown who looked into her magic glasses and pretended, like Jerry Dunphy, to recognize her viewers, as she read the names of birthday kids whose parents had sent in post cards. She kind of scared me.

Now I've nearly finished college, done my week in jail (time served), and am working the streets of Los Angeles as a paid canvasser for the first "Jobs With Peace" (Proposition X) campaign, supervised by a trio of now legendary Los Angeles progressive activists—Larry Frank, a tall, thin white guy from a religious family, Anthony Thigpenn, a tall, thin Black guy who'd worked on an early signature campaign for a civilian review board after the police killed Eulah Love, and Sharon Dulugich, a beautiful, curly-haired white woman with a last name ending like mine—ich. These three are young, smart, and brave. I work my heart out for them. Paychecks, tiny symbolic things, are signed by the Southern Christian Leadership Council's Mark Ridley Thomas, later a city council member. The office on Vermont is broken into, petitions stolen. We start over.

My canvassing partner, Maggie, is an Irish national who's come to the States to work for nuclear disarmament, met an American, stayed. She doesn't drive. In a few months, we visit nearly every part of the city. We go to South Central to collect signatures on the day-aid checks that arrive in the mail, standing next to frozen meat vans and Nation of Islam recruiters. We set up on the Venice boardwalk, in Westwood, and near Farmer's Market.

Then we are off for lucrative half-days at the Gelson's in Pacific Palisades, where rich people often decline to sign the petition but slip a five or ten dollar bill into our donations coffee can. The air is salty, cool. On our way home, we pull over on PCH and watch the sunset. I sleep first on my parents' couch in Downey, then on a friend's floor in Oakwood, then find a tiny room with no bathroom in a broken-down old mansion on the beach in Santa Monica. I have one "incomplete" to finish to earn a degree in Comparative Literature, and an understanding, for perhaps the first time, of the proportions here, of poverty to wealth, freeway to boulevard, war to peace. I am also beginning to understand how forbidden it is to acknowledge these, to speak about them.

My all-time favorite street canvassing moment: I approach a fiftyish white woman at Westwood and Galey, near the entrance to UCLA, offering my pitch about a petition to transform our military economy to a peacetime one. This is a tourist spot, good for donations; also good for signatures because it's supposedly liberal. She looks like my mother. I ask if she's registered to vote in LA. "Yes." I ask her, again, if she'll help us reduce military spending in LA.

She looks me, and says confidently, "Oh, my husband takes care of that."

Back at the office I joke that I've met the First Lady, Nancy Reagan.

Years later, when the verdict in Simi Valley is announced, I recall that woman, confident that her Mister is taking care of things.

In the days that follow the riots, armored personnel trucks roll up and down Ocean Avenue in Santa Monica, past the Rand Corporation and Palisades Park, the Camera Obscura and high-rise hotels. My wife and I stand on the Santa Monica Pier, watching the exodus of the Westside by its affluent residents, red tail lights making their way up PCH.

On Monday I drive back to Orange County.

Downey is famous for Apollo capsules and the Carpenters singing duo. For a car dealership slogan: "Where the freeways meet in Downey." Indeed, the city is bordered on all sides. It sounds like a giant lock combination: 91, 5, 605, 710. There is a highway, and a fairly constant parade of men in gurneys, of patients staggering by on crutches, of kids my own age strapped in wheelchairs with metal pins in their heads, of spinal cord injury patients and the last generation of polio epidemic victims. They are paralyzed, they cannot move right. Stiff. On any afternoon, you see them dressed in white hospital gowns, rolling down the sidewalk on Imperial, on their way to Beach's Market to buy cigarettes and liquor and candy. Some will live their entire lives at Rancho. They are our neighbors.

The week of the riots, I am teaching composition to the college children of Korean-American shopkeepers who bail on class before I do, needing to help their parents defend their liquor stores, grocery stores, and warehouses, they say.

"It's like a war," says one of my students. "Isn't it?"

Proposition X, "Jobs with Peace," required the City Council to ask President Reagan and Congress to spend less on "defense" and more on social programs. It directed the City Council to study the amount of federal taxes from Los Angeles spent on "defense" and the effect on LA if half that were spent on local social programs. It proposed cutting "defense" spending by about $145 billion from $293 billion.

The quotation marks, above, are mine: "defense." It's like war: Militarism. First Strike. Evil Empire. Unilateral spending which, during Mrs. Reagan's husband's term, represents the largest peacetime military spending in history and, elegantly enough, the largest transfer of public wealth to private ownership.

I recall those Russian spacemen quietly signing dollar bills at Rockwell and patting my little brother's head. And the wealthy Palisades liberals who filled our coffee can. And that day of civil disobedience, with my father and all the Hughes employees standing on the second floor, watching us get arrested.

Prop X actually won. Yes: 61%. No: 30%. It produced the study, finding what the activists said it would, only worse: federal money was going to Palmdale, Chatsworth, Pasadena, replacing industrial jobs in LA—which had once employed minorities—with military and aerospace—which employed whites.

I call my old boss Larry Frank to get this part right.

"They wanted to jump start, the economy," says Larry, "but they completely undercut the civilian industrial base to appeal to white voters."

Larry Frank has an analysis, and I am not going to be able to hang up without getting all of it.

"The destruction of the Black Panther Party," Larry informs me, "the introduction of crack cocaine, the closing of rubber and steel plants, then the scapegoating of drug criminals. Substitute young urban Black men for communists and then look, later, at who funded Three Strikes: The California Correctional Peace Officers Association."

I ask him my big question. Could "Jobs With Peace" have saved us from riots? "You're being too ambitious," he says. "But if you're looking for a thesis, I'll say that the verdict and the riots showed us who was in charge."

As we exit the big Food 4 Less warehouse, my friend Elena, a civil rights attorney, arrives. She's found the only photocopy store open for miles, somewhere over in Boyle Heights, and waits in the parking lot, passing out literature to whomever will take it after a day of cheerless grocery bagging. Two Security guys emerge from the grocery warehouse, threatening to call the cops if she doesn't stop. Their warning seems half-hearted. Calling the police doesn't seem likely somehow, not now.

"The industry," they call it. It surrounds us, even as most of us don't see it in our daily lives. Then, one day, you are a kid riding your bike through a hospital and it is there, on the back of a pickup truck, illuminated with carbon arc lights and big white reflector parasols: a guy pretending to be a wounded vet in a wheelchair, surrounded by real people in wheelchairs.

Naturally, you could mistake the industry for the movies.

We cannot talk about the real industry. It's not on TV. Security is waiting to stop us or somebody's husband is in charge or Jerry Dunphy is being robbed or Marines are being bombed. The real industry is connected by a world-famous freeway system. Some of the real industry is adjacent the airport, on El Segundo Boulevard. It's the first thing you see as you land there, over on the left, all in a row. The real industry is buried in huge concrete bunkers off the San Diego Freeway, under acres of open field, which we cannot confirm or deny.

I figured it out in driver's ed, at Warren High School in Downey. A bunch of teenagers got into a car with an instructor, who drove us over to that Rockwell parking lot on a Saturday morning and told us to follow the lines painted on the asphalt.

Southern California is laid out in a big grid, highlighted as in Thomas Brothers maps, only in white, brown, and black. Like the electric train set diorama Dad built for my brother and me, plywood with tracks and little plastic houses, all the streets painted at right angles, a train going round and round forever until it skips off the track.

The day the riots began it's all made too obvious and, yes, embarrassing. The strangers driving on the freeway, staring straight ahead, cannot make eye contact. They talk to their passengers, to their kids in the back seat, without moving their heads, without turning around. Their fingers grip the wheel tightly, and only their lips move. They seem to be checking their rearview mirrors.

168

TALKIN' BOUT A REVOLUTION

David L. Ulin

"Tonight the riots begin on the back streets of America."
—Tracy Chapman

The night four white Los Angeles police officers were acquitted of assault in the videotaped beating of black motorist Rodney King, I was busy trying to save a baby bird in my front yard. I had noticed it on the way home that afternoon—a brown and white lump of feathers and flesh no bigger than a golf ball, squawking in fear and hunger on the lip of the lawn. I called the LA Animal Hotline, where they told me it was probably a starling, and that if they came out to pick it up, the bird would be destroyed. If I wanted to rescue it myself, that was my business, but baby starlings needed to be fed once an hour, every hour, for six or eight weeks, at the end of which time, if the creature even survived, I would most likely have myself a pet, utterly dependent upon me to provide for its welfare and totally unprepared to be returned to the wild.

Not knowing quite what to do, I made up a mixture of cereal and milk, and went downstairs where, after a bit of struggle, I actually got the terrified bird to eat. I was feeling pretty good about myself, thinking about what a new experience this was—born and raised in Manhattan, a resident of Los Angeles for less than a year, I'd never even seen a baby bird before, outside of a classroom or a zoo—thinking that, in spite of all my reservations about the place, LA wasn't so bad when you got right down to it. Sure, it was too spread out, even segregated, with no real sense of community to speak of; sure, it was a city that seemed somehow unfocused, the result, I had decided, of its slow-paced residential lifestyle, its strange combination of the suburban and the surreal. But watching the bird and listening to the rustle of leaves in the evening breeze, I found myself understanding for the first time that maybe, just maybe, that was part of the point. As darkness started to descend and the night began to grow chill, I knelt there on the grass, almost forgetting I was in a city at all.

That's a moment I keep thinking about, a moment that won't leave me alone. It's a moment that doesn't make sense to me, or perhaps one that makes too much sense, that says too much about the disparity between the haves and the have-nots in this country, and particularly in the city of LA. For, at the very instant I was experiencing my epiphany on the lawn, intersections in South Central Los Angeles—less than ten miles away—were already beginning to ignite in response to the King verdict like lit fuses, fuses that before they were extinguished would detonate much of this scattered city, destroying not only property and lives but also the myth of Los Angeles as a multi-cultural human mosaic, a place where the old antagonisms of race and culture simply do not apply. By the time the rioting and the looting finally ended, the whole status quo here—the status quo that, until then, had allowed white middle-class residents like myself to live with the tacit understanding that LA was somehow different than other American cities—had been cast completely into doubt, although it remains to be seen if those doubts will lead to any new ideas of how to heal our divisions, or whether they'll just be too much for us to deal with, another reason for those of us who still can to stick our heads even deeper into the sand.

Of course, all our protestations to the contrary, Los Angeles has been a city beset with deep racial divisions for years—since before the Watts riots in 1965, riots that were quelled but never dealt with, riots that destroyed communities which have never been rebuilt. Unlike Watts, the riots this time were not unexpected, although the widespread nature of the violence took everybody by surprise. The first night, that baby bird on my lawn now irrevocably forgotten, I watched live helicopter coverage as the city slowly descended into chaos. Downtown, protesters stormed Police Headquarters and tried to set fire to City Hall. Sitting with my wife in front of the television, I thought about how much this looked like an insurrection, about how I'd never before seen an American seat of government under siege. In an odd kind of way, it was exhilarating, proof that these things could happen here, that even in America, where the existence of inequity had been denied by a government that seemed to have lost all its compassion for the dispossessed, there was a time when people would stand up and say, "Enough!" I felt a surge of sympathy and adrenaline sweep through me as I wondered where it would end.

Then the cameras switched back to South Central to show live coverage of a white man being pulled out of his Chevy Bronco and beaten in the middle of the street by members of a frenzied mob, an image so terrifying, so at odds with the veneer of civility to which we are accustomed, that it was almost impossible to grasp what was going on. For the first time, I began to feel fear—fear of disorder, fear of the mob, fear of being the wrong color in a place and time where that was a capital offense. As the helicopter-borne cameras panned across the neighborhood, I could see several fires starting to burn. The most popular targets seemed to be large commercial buildings, the kind that looked like they had once been used as warehouses or storerooms, but were now devoted primarily to swap meets, where hundreds of small-scale entrepreneurs set up makeshift stalls of goods. Old wood-frame constructions, they burned quickly, viciously. The cameras took it all in, including the lack of any police or fire department presence to help bring the chaos under control.

The absence of the law was ironic to say the least, since one of the first things I'd ever noticed about Los Angeles was the sheer volume of so-called peace officers who normally patrolled its streets. Not all of them were LAPD—there was also the Los Angeles County Sheriff's Department, the California Highway Patrol, the Beverly Hills Police, and various transit cops, private security guards, and other armed and uniformed authorities—but the sense I'd come to have was almost one of living in a police state, where major thoroughfares like Hollywood Boulevard were closed to prevent cruising on Saturday nights, and looking suspicious was reason enough to be stopped. The official line was that certain restrictions were necessary to keep a handle on the gang problem, but if you watched the cops closely, it was obvious that something else was going on as well. There was a glint in their eyes, the glint of too much unchallenged power, a glint that Rodney King had surely seen the night he'd tried to outrun them and fallen victim instead to the brunt of their batons.

Yet Wednesday night, as parts of Los Angeles started to burn in earnest, the police were nowhere to be found. In some cases, it would be more than two hours before they arrived on the scene. Later, Daryl Gates, LA's embattled Chief of Police, would claim the delay in response had been intentional, so as not to stir up the anger of the black community, for whom the King beating and verdict had become just the latest symbols of the brutality and racism of the LAPD. But Gates' explanation didn't make sense, for reticence had never been part of his approach to law enforcement—he was, after all, the man who had once sipped tea with Nancy Reagan in a trailer while a police SWAT team staged a raid on a crack house outside, and among his best-known public statements was one opining that "casual drug users should be taken out and shot." a comment that, in the wake of the King fiasco, appeared on posters all over town beneath an image of the Chief with the word "shot" changed to "beaten."

The police finally did make their presence known, but by then things were already out of control. On the Hollywood Freeway, just west of downtown, a mob stopped traffic and then set fire to several palm trees that lined the roadway. South Central was starting to look like Kuwait, with plumes of thick black smoke spiraling into the night sky from fires that kept blossoming like wild flowers. At a midnight press conference in Sacramento, California Governor Pete Wilson announced he was activating the National Guard, a decision that would later be questioned when the first two thousand Guardsmen arrived without ammunition, more than twenty-four hours after they were supposed to have been deployed.

It wasn't until Thursday that most of white Los Angeles got directly involved. That morning, things were calm enough for the

Fire Department to announce a lull in the destruction. My wife went to the health club to work out, and I set up a lunchtime appointment at a hotel in in Beverly Hills. Driving over there at one o'clock, I noticed a couple of groups of black teenagers descending on San Vicente Boulevard, not too far from my apartment. I found myself wondering what they were doing here, then, almost immediately, felt deeply ashamed. It was the same type of stereotyping the police engaged in, the residue of bigotry I'd never been able to get away from. I turned on the radio, but everything seemed quiet, so I put those kids out of my mind and continued on my way.

At the hotel, it was like a different world. In the lobby, matrons sat and talked quietly over tea, while up in the health spa, where my meeting was to take place, people lounged by the open pool, sleeping in the sun. The whole thing reminded me of pictures I'd seen of Saigon before the fall—the colonialists sipping gin in the sanctity of a hotel bar while all around them the city raged—except here, there wasn't even the mentality of a siege. Everyone seemed so unaffected, so utterly unaware. The night before, I'd half-jokingly told my wife that if the rioters wanted to get something done, they should head for Beverly Hills and hit the rich people where they lived; now, I understood in a fundamental way just how true that was. As long as the people with the money were immune, all the destruction in the world wouldn't serve to change anything. These people didn't care; they didn't have to.

The atmosphere had changed by the time my meeting ended, at around 2:30. The pool area was empty of guests, and the only employee I ran into told me that "they" were coming towards Beverly Hills. When I got outside, I was assaulted by the dual smells of tar and fire; to the east, the sky was filled with wisps of acrid black smoke. With traffic at a near-standstill on the major streets, panic was starting to set in. All the way home, I looked at the faces in the cars around me—white faces, terrified faces. Whether they were trying to get out of town or just home to their families it was impossible to tell, but they were moving with the mentality of the mob, a mob on the run this time, but a mob all the same. The fear was everywhere, it was contagious, when we stopped at red lights, we would all look to see who was in the cars around us, ready to drive on at the slightest provocation. The radio was reporting looting at the Beverly Center, a huge upscale mall not ten blocks from where I lived, and as I turned onto La Cienega Boulevard, I noticed that the mini-mall where, the day before, I had dropped off some xeroxing was going up in flames.

All in all, it took me about an hour to get to my apartment, a trip of no more than three or four miles. I was lucky. My brother, a law student at UCLA, spent three hours that afternoon driving the ten miles from school to home, and a friend of mine spent an hour and a half trying to get from Burbank to Hollywood, a drive that normally would take fifteen minutes. By mid-afternoon, the entire city had shut down, and with a dusk-to-dawn curfew in effect for the night, it appeared things would stay that way for a while. My block was peaceful enough that a woman lay out in a patch of sunlight on the grass across the street, but the air was full of sirens rushing in every direction, and any remaining illusions I may have had as to my own security ended when, about ten minutes after I got home, my next door neighbor came by to see if I was all right.

"Do you have protection for your home?" he asked me.

I looked at him blankly, wondering what he meant.

"A gun," he said. "I can lend you one if you need it."

My first thought was that he was kidding, but after taking a close look at his face, I knew it wasn't the case.

"Thanks," I said, "but I don't think I could shoot anybody. It'd probably only get me killed."

"You sure?" he said.

I nodded.

"Okay," he told me. "But the offer's open, in case you change your mind."

I watched him as he headed back to his apartment, then went inside and started calling around town to make sure everyone I knew was okay. Phone service was intermittent at best. I had a nightmare flash of what would happen if someone broke into the apartment and we couldn't get the lines to work to call for help, but I quickly realized that it wouldn't matter anyway—the police were so overextended already just dealing with the rioting that there would be no officers left to deal with domestic problems like that, and even

if there were, the news was telling me that emergency services operators couldn't even answer all the calls. For a moment, I considered
rethinking my neighbor's offer of protection, before putting the idea
out of my head once and for all.

By the time I got off the phone, any excitement or sympathy I'd
had towards the rioters the night before had been replaced by a
numbing exhaustion that left little room for thought. Watching the
news, where cameras were now following the fires that were taking
out business after business in Koreatown, I even felt a sense of shame
at my exhilaration of the previous night. The honest rage that had
sparked the rioting had now degenerated into little more than a
form of tribalism, with resentments and antagonisms which had
simmered between minority communities for too long being played
out on the kangaroo court of the streets. When the television
showed a posse of Korean businessmen taking up positions on
Vermont Avenue with Uzis, shotguns, and other heavy artillery, I
didn't know whose side I was on anymore.

One thing I did know was that I didn't buy the characteriza-
tions—promulgated by both the media and the police—of the looters as a bunch of thugs and hoodlums. Doubtless, that was a part of
it, but I had seen enough images on TV of young men and women
emerging from convenience stores clutching packages of diapers or
tubes of toothpaste to recognize that at least some of the looting was
being done out of necessity, a necessity that made me feel uncom-
fortable all over again. For as the rioting progressed, I had come to
understand that I, too, was complicit—a well-heeled liberal from a
nice, although not too nice, part of town, who liked the idea of revolution as long as it didn't occur too close to home. Now, with my
neighborhood liquor store looted, and fires burning along Beverly
Boulevard, within walking distance of my apartment, I was hiding
behind locked doors, checking the street every couple of minutes to
see if there was anything untoward going on, monitoring the
progress of the devastation on television and hoping that it would
come no closer than it already had.

I spent all of Thursday night that way, lights out to keep my windows from becoming a target. With the National Guard in the
streets, it was obvious that this night would be the night, that if the
city could make it through the darkness without any more major
damage, we would probably be okay. My wife, overloaded by the

violence and the tension, went to bed early, but I sat up, peering outside whenever I heard a car go by. The curfew was supposedly holding, and the fires had lessened, but sirens still screamed in the distance, and the newscasters still reported a number of new blazes. In Koreatown, a sniper took a few shots at some National Guardsmen; the rumor was that one of the vigilante businessmen might have gotten out of hand. It was impossible to tell, there were too many guns on the streets, and everyone was worried about the civilians who were out there packing weapons and had nobody to answer to but themselves.

Friday morning, it felt as if a tenuous peace had at last been reached. After checking out the news to make sure it was safe, my wife and I took a drive to see what was going on. At the Beverly Center, stores were open; we popped in and rented a couple of videos, then continued on our way. On certain corners, it was as if nothing had ever happened—people drinking coffee at a sidewalk cafe—while at others, it looked like a war zone, complete with soldiers in battle fatigues, carrying automatic weapons. Cruising down La Brea Avenue, past the husk of what had once been Samy's Camera, we noticed a private security officer cradling a carbine on the roof of a furniture store, and other armed guards at the entrance to Ralph's market, where a long line of shoppers waited to get inside. Later, we headed for Vermont Avenue, in the heart of Koreatown, to see what had happened over there. It was both better and worse than we'd expected—better because huge sections of the city had come through the firestorm unscathed, worse because the sight of so much damage was gut-wrenching to confront face-to-face. Watching the destruction on television, there had been a side of me which believed in some fanciful way that it was happening somewhere else; now, I knew those feelings for the wishful thoughts they were, and understood that I had been here for an apocalyptic moment, one that had scarred thousands of people far worse than it had me.

For all intents and purposes, the rioting was over by Friday afternoon, although the curfew remained in effect throughout the weekend, and the National Guard is still here as I write these lines. So quickly did things return to some semblance of normality that by Saturday, I was being invited to a post-riot celebration, curfew be damned. I declined, but the ease with which white Los Angeles—my

Los Angeles—got over the events of those forty-eight hours is unsettling in the extreme. It was as if, as soon as the fires were put out in our neighborhoods, we allowed ourselves to slip into some kind of collective amnesia, as if these riots had nothing to do with us.

But they did, and they do. America, as the Kerner Commission predicted after the last wave of urban rioting in the late 1960s, has become two distinct countries, separate and unequal, with the division based on race. And every one of us who lives here is equally to blame. In the week or so since the violence abated, there's been a lot of talk about rebuilding the hardest hit neighborhoods, about offering tax breaks for businesses who might want to invest in South Central LA. That's fine—in fact, that's great. But the problems that face us will never be solved until we can find a way to re-integrate the members of the underclass—whatever race they may be—into the mainstream of society.

And that's a tall order. Already, I've heard jokes from friends about building a wall around the predominantly white westside of Los Angeles, and letting everyone whose home or business falls on the outside fend for themselves. That's the logic behind a place like Beverly Hills, which, surrounded on all sides by LA proper, is, by law, a municipality unto itself, with its own government, and a tax base that funnels nothing into the greater city of which it is a part. But if anything good can come out of these riots, it must be the realization that all of us in Los Angeles live in the same community, that, whether in South Central or Koreatown or Hollywood or Beverly Hills, we share the same city, good and bad. That's an idea which is truly revolutionary, the kind of idea that could transform LA into the type of city that, until the trouble started, the people here liked to believe it was. For we cannot protect ourselves from each other; the ease with which the violence spread from neighborhood to neighborhood is irrefutable proof of that. We are all responsible, and we must learn to think collectively, to care for each other as we care for ourselves. Or, in the words of Rodney King, whose impassioned news conference on Friday afternoon may have had a great deal to do with the coming of the peace, to "get along."

178

STOOP SONAR

Marco Villalobos

sometimes the drums just stop but the street still hums a bass line

from myrtle ave

feet kick past / choreographed

all on beat

car horns honk at you / on cue

whistles from bodegas

erupt spontaneous

soundtrack to weekend

evening

original jams

past & present time

natural metronomes emerge from stone / faces

stay out in darkness / sound

new womb music make 757 shake

break

sonic boom in flaps of silence

in cracked slabs of silence in slaps

of measured silence

Sirens

indicate tendencies toward violence

and fill the air with tension extracted from apprehension

not to mention

past incidents of insurrection.

Riots

quieted by projectiles

coincidental missiles

firebomb explode through kitchen window

sunday dinner. condolences to grieving widows

smoke cleared away

by martial law

shots volley—10 o'clock.

papi, a donde vas? where you going mama?

people stay inside

make sure they got the doors locked

On the boulevard—soldiers

lined up for seven blocks

Battle armor tanks and tear gas

graffiti clean up

movie stars sweep up
the broken glass emergencies
of the present swiftly slip
into the past,

until

the next

reaction

All
we doin is defendin

182

I was at SC when shit hit the fan. I was there for the worst of it, then a couple of friends dragged my ass out of there on the third day and took me to this condo in Marina Del Rey, where I was basically surrounded by pretty rich white people who you could tell none of that horror and strife mattered a damn to them. We all got pretty drunk (I think I left some T-Bird in the freezer—T-Bird which someone had bought for irony's sake—so that in the morning all that cheap booze had soaked down the baguettes and shit in the fridge. Who knew that short dogs popped when you froze them? Irony's a bitch.). Anyway, I was there, and by the fourth day, when the Guard was sent in, I was back at SC, hanging out at this donut shop near the 32nd Street Market, watching these guys in cammies chowing down on jelly-filleds with their empty M-16s slung from their shoulders(Remember how the Guard wasn't allowed to have loaded clips in their rifles?).

I was there with an old friend of mine, Wally, (really cool as in sincere and good-hearted, because he liked to wear pukka shells, which is decidely uncool) a white kid from Pasadena who wanted to find that clean-up group Edward James Olmos started. He kept talking about this, trying to get me to say something about it, as in,

Am I going to help out or not? But, I was just quiet, trying to eat my donut. Basically, I was thinking "You're not going to do shit and neither am I," but like I said, Wally was (I'm guessing he still is; we've lost touch) a really cool guy, so I thought it best to not say anything.

And then a bunch of other shit happened, too, like cruising around Koreatown and South Central with my friend Roy in his Honda, which was amazing in lots of ways, but mostly in that it didn't occur to me till we were around Pico Rivera and there were all these homeboys in black mesh tank tops with white wife-beaters underneath, holding up golf clubs and metal poles over their heads, that my good friend Roy was Korean, and oh fuck, you know how that goes.

HELICOPTERS SWINGING IN THE BLOOD

Scott Wannberg

Do you remember the rinse cycle of '65

when Watts made the headlines

Six days of torches, broken glass, skulls

A commission wheeled itself in and wrote some words

Pay attention to this tragedy, it sang

Pay attention to the have-nots for they are singing

on your washlines and your temperature just might not

be able to feel good when the wallpaper snarls in

traffic.

back in '65 I was 12 years old

they got a tower in Watts

and they say its a mighty strong one

27 years up the path

around the sorry bend

that tower maybe is still a mighty strong one

but something snapped on the vertebrae of the hey now

something never seemingly got put together

and here it is, 1992

and bigger than Rodney King

bigger than a jury in Simi

bigger and harsher and more painful

here in 1992

nobody has learned anyone

no one has figured all that much

back in '65 a commission wheeled itself onto the front porch

pay attention, it snapped

your inner cities are festering, they are wounded, they

are tired of not being seen

here we go then

in the merry-go-round's dark language

business as usual

drive by shootings, gang killings

drug deals on the corner, unemployment, single parent

homes barely breathing, business is as usual here

in South Central

this forgotten patch that nobody muttered about when

the Olympics came to play here years ago

when they named part of the airport after Tom Bradley

down here the killing is a daily song

the old Jewish merchant class now replaced by the Koreans,

the new merchant class

who have no idea of the history and pain of

the inner workings of the city.

I watched Koreans become targets

last week

in the relative clam of my West Side

white apartment

I sat with a lousy cold, watching my city explode.

Helicopters danced in the angry sky

showing motorists being pulled from cars and beaten

motorists who probably didn't buy the King verdict

given a chance to say so

but it was beyond the King thing

it was beyond the Korean thing

it was all down the line payback punch up son

it was break out and kick some ass no matter what ass

it was fuck it we are tired and dead and done

and nobody sees us anyhow

unless we go mad in the dancing sun of love

unless we go mad and begin to tear

at anyone and anything

here we are at Normandie and Florence

no police in sight

not that long ago Gates the prophet said he would be

ready for anything

I got the men I got the money I got the connectives

here at Normandie and Florence at Tom's liquors

looted and burned

the fires began to wave

look at us city

lok at how far we can spread

how easy the fabric burns

were you in the screening room

then were you in a safe chair watching

it all implode and explode and

hello

city of the angels with a wounded ticket

the late show is very very scary and tense

it's not a race thing, this verdict

everyone said there is no race thing

but the race is on

the race is fleeing and fleeting

in the city of the angels

in the city of humming guns

the white news anchors all looked tense

we got a situation at Parker Center

the very center of Chief Parker of '65

who ruled with an iron fist

where is Chief Darryl oh he's in Brentwood at a fête

he's being honored

oh honorable one

there are victims being taken down in your city of love

oh honorable chief

where are your men and resources now

oh Mayor oh my dancing academy

can you chart a course that will get us safe to the

next new planet

where everyone can have a paycheck

where everyone can be allowed to breathe and sing

without undue duress

I sat in the relative calm of my white apartment

and the smoke and the flames and the pain

outdid Cosby

outdid Amazing Stories and Most Wanted

did you go back as far as '65

this will never ever happen again

we learn from our painful mistakes

where will they build the Florence and Normandie tower

will they build it on top of the Griffith Park observatory

so we can see it coming the next time

and the Crips and the Bloods get together to either

try and learn to live with each other or to take on

the police take your pick

is taking on the police learning to live with

each other?

here in the tense end of love

here in the whirling blender hotel of

mixed motives and mistaken gestures

doublepark your soul

the Sunday hacks are now riding through second guessing

and blaming

Bush wants to dig up LBJ's corpse and lay it on him

when in fact the Vietnam thing pulled LBJ off something

that actually was working when it came to the faces

of American painful cities

the Vietnam thing that Nixon picked up and then

Cambodia taking the money away from American streets

taking away from your American streets can cost you in

the end

and now it's time to bail out Russia

god bless them for they hunger

it's time to spread the money throughout Europe and Asia

but when the police get a complaint or call

in South Central they don't bother to go look

death as usual

hello

as usual

drive by loving

can cost you

in the long run

Bill Clinton with his thumb up

next to a burned out store

all the dreams charred and blackened

by rage

all the dreams learning to try and hobble

in the post apocalyptic a.m. of

yes we go the Guard and the Marines

to guard us from our own brothers and sisters

it got Fredericks of Hollywood

and Sammy's Camera it spread out of where it should have
stayed cause we all figure if its only that neighborhood
well they get what they deserve
but White Flight don't you know settled in
and the suburb guns came down off the wall and
the hip folks took off in a panic
leaving their city to maybe smolder
into oblivion
hello my children, did I say it would be easy, in
the sad arguments of who we are, and a few days
ago after the inherent rage and madness, a contingent
went to Simi Valley to protest the verdict, you do
remember the verdict that triggered this painting
the one Nathaniel West wrote of in Day of the Locust
the burning of LA
in Simi Valley a full grown white woman who should have
known better enough to halfway understand pointed at a black
woman and said We don't want you burning down our homes Go
Away. Let us Live our Life, our life to be lived
is some kind of love some kind of empathy in the shooting
gallery tonsils of the moment. the woman had not come to
burn anyone's house down, but there it is, because she had
to say it, because she even thought it
the wheel is bleeding the wheel is lost help me turn the
wheel oh help me struggle in the fearful streets of our
hearts help me learn to see
as I walk barefoot on the glass and the species and this

inevitable species of pain reaches out

Edward James Olmos with a broom help me sweep away the

detritus and phleghm siphoning off the human heart

sweep me along these singing seeming streets. hear it sadly,

the death toll now 58, ah but every week in the hod the

death rate averages at least 10, the hood of human sways

unsteady in the precarious latitude of longing

the have-nots break and burn and loot, blacks, whites,

hispanics, looting blacks, whites, hispanics, asians

what movie is this? didn't we see this thing in '65 except

maybe with less Asians? I saw this

actor before, he held a

cocktail in his right, not left hand, the rage is a rhythm

do not deny it, do not hide it or

sweep it under, do not dig up dead Texans and lay

it on them, the rage is here and the

rage is now, meet it, face it, learn it, deal with it,

dance with it

the helicopters of the bloodstream are confused, they go all

over trying to figure a trade,

the helicopters of the bloodstream need an interpreter

here tonight in this strange strange world

I reach out and say, the hood is the heart

and the boys and the girls of it all must learn

to pay attention in order to follow the dance

down to where it all must somehow

mean something.

RIDING THE BOX

Ellery Washington C.

I must have been on the phone with an HBO rep, or with Showtime, or The Movie Channel, or someone like that—I was still in cable television then—when I first heard the sirens. The television in my office was on, it was always on, a strange kind of perk; and the rep in my ear was going on and on about some kind of sales promotion, a new cable show, or some other marketing thing that quite frankly didn't interest me at all. The sirens, however, did. They startled me. Swiveling around in my chair to see the screen, I excused myself from the call, fumbled through the mess that was typically my desk, and then—as if the ambulatory screams weren't already loud enough—frisked the television remote to turn the volume up. There, leaning into a wide-lens camera was a rather large balding man in an ill-fitting, short-sleeved Polo shirt—much too small, the color of which I can no longer remember—and khaki pants. An impressionistic blur of red, yellow, and black chaos flickered behind him creating a violent backdrop to his unusually stoic voice and manner. The entire scene was being broadcast from a large open lot near the corner of Pico Boulevard and Vermont Avenue.

Evidently, a little more than an hour before my HBO promo call, a series of Not Guilty verdicts had been handed down by the Simi

Valley jury in all of the counts against the four officers charged in the Rodney King motorist trial. Various incidents of physical violence and property destruction had already begun to "spark out," as the newscaster put it, "around the city. Primarily in the Hollywood, downtown, and South Central areas. Though surely"—a dramatic pause—"the violence would spread."

Men and women ran back and forth, lighting fires, smashing store windows, stopping cars on the street. I watched these skycam images and graphics with a profound sense of disbelief and dread. Seized by a sudden fear, I couldn't move. What in God's name was happening out there? Then—yes, a reflex thought. Out there. At that moment I was not 'out there.' I wasn't really even in Los Angeles, but safely inside my Santa Monica office, standing behind my desk, leaning against my hunter green, brushed leather chair. The melee, smoke, and growing flames were, at that moment, contained within the nineteen-inch screen mounted above the file cabinet, as far away from me then as anything else that ever entered the room through that wide black box. As horrifying as they were, these were not the worst images to have flashed across that screen. This was simply TV. Or so my disbelief tried to tell me. I was safe. Only just as I'd finally managed to slow my rapid breathing down, Dionci, my young, temporary assistant, burst into my office in tears.

"I've got to get home!" she screamed.

Dionci was twenty-four and black. She had a six-year-old son and lived in Los Angeles just off South Normandie Avenue and Adams Street, near the epicenter of one of the very first sparks. She had worked in the secretarial pool six months before—as an act of company policy—she, along with the rest of the office secretaries, received a fifty-cent an hour raise and officially became administrative assistants. Two weeks after the mass promotion she was given a temporary assignment to work with me and my permanent assistant in marketing where I too had been freshly promoted, though fortunately my promotion to Regional Marketing Manager carried with it a bit more than a fifty-cent boost in salary.

Cable Television had just fallen under the grip of a new FCC-congressional reregulation act that levied substantial pressure on all cable operators to lower programming rates and to increase operator quality commitments to their customers. Amid these congressional demands, my company was—of course—taking the opportunity of forced change to restructure the entire service such that we could actually increase our profits—substantially at that—and side-step the new guidelines. "Tiers of Service," more choices, greater flexibility, was the corporate slogan. "Tiers" basically meant that what had once been a bulk product of "basic service" cable channels was to be broken up into a variety of smaller "packaged" services, each with an individual price. In short, it was a slick way of getting our customers to pay the same price—give or take a few cents—for what amounted to about half the product without risking any retribution under the new FCC cable laws. A clever hole. While making the strategic decision to create these new "Tiers" seemed a rather quick and painless one on the part of the East coast situated corporate office, disguising such a consumer costly deception during a time when subscribers were expecting some kind of rebate required a little extra marketing help.

For that I was promoted and given Dionci. Considering my region covered many of the most influential, media-savvy, and demanding areas of Los Angeles (Santa Monica, West Hollywood, Brentwood, Bel Air, and Beverly Hills to name a few) the addition of a single new temporary assistant fell well below the magnitude of assistance I had expected. Dionci, however, was a great help. She worked long hours, was extremely conscientious, and appeared—even under the most stressful of deadlines—levelheaded. She simply never got upset. Which was why her complete and utter panic the afternoon of the riots overtook me. As she stood there crying in the doorway, I suddenly felt that I too had to get out of that office and head home as quickly as possible.

Looking back at it now, I suppose the reason that the explosion of violence directly following the Rodney King trial verdict came to me as such a surprise was that I had simply stopped thinking about the trial. Or maybe stopped worrying about it is more accurate to say. I had so many other, more pressing concerns. My overly possessive lover, for instance. My new home—we'd only just moved from a shared apartment in Hollywood to a much larger, beachside place in Long Beach. And then there was the job, I was suddenly important. Still, all this considered, my relative lack of interest in the trial by the time of the verdict was furthered by the very element, which might have, in the minds of most people around me, kept it in the forefront of my mind. I, like Rodney King, am a black man, and—

give or take a few years and possibly a pound or two—the same age, general build, and hue. Surely what happened to him could have happened to me. But then, that was exactly it, wasn't it?—the reason I had not followed the trial with the same fervor as many other non-black people I knew and worked with. What had kept the Rodney King trial, as well as that graphically violent video tape, running in the minds of so many others was the shock of it. And I wasn't shocked at all. I, like many other African-American men, had already been the subject of police harassment on more than one occasion. The most memorable of which being not long before the first broadcast of the Rodney King beating video.

It was a Thursday night, almost midnight, and having returned home from a movie in Century City—"Jungle Fever," by Spike Lee no less—I decided to step back out, grab a quick cup of coffee, and see if a friend of mine was, as he had told me he would be, hanging out at a local bar. I lived in West Hollywood then, on Laurel Avenue near the corner of Fountain and Crescent Heights, which meant I was in one of the few Angeleno neighborhoods in which I could actually walk to local restaurants and bars. It did, however, usually mean a walk down Santa Monica Boulevard, which was, at that time, heavily patrolled by the local sheriffs department and police. It was the beginning of a crackdown on prostitution. Los Angeles Police patrols covered the heavily solicited neighborhoods between Vine Street and La Brea Avenue, the West Hollywood Sheriffs department took over from there. The gay male cruising scene on the streets sur-rounding The Circus Bookstore was reputed and dense, and the police kept a special eye on the adjacent parking lots and alleyways. Though that particular block was not known for a frequency of prostitution traffic, the general crack-down created a perfect excuse for the sheriffs to make their presence strongly felt in the neighbor-hood as a deterrent to what was considered by the more affluent members of that particular community "lewd behavior." I conclud-ed later that the word "lewd" might on occasion also be applied to just about any black man between the ages of eighteen and thirty-five caught going out for coffee after eleven p.m.

I'd barely made it out of my front door when a black-and-white police car soared down the street past me, then, two buildings up from mine, came to a screeching halt. The driver hit reverse, revved his way back in my direction, then struck the breaks a second time.

I spun around to look behind me—no one was there—then back to face the squad car. Two tall, white law-enforcement officers, poised as if they were sitting on invisible floating chairs, held their guns out in front of them, both pointed directly at me. It took no orders to make me raise my hands and freeze as one of the officers, the thinner of the two (dark brown hair and a well-clipped mustache), made his way toward me. His gun lead the approach, a divining rod and I, water. Fortunately for me, I was wearing a blue-striped oxford shirt, khaki pants, and loafers, rather than a karate suit, or baggy jeans, or shiny jogging pants, or a thick gold chain, or anything else for that matter that would have indicated that I might put up a fight. My somewhat casually mannered dress, however, did not dissuade the officer from pushing me up against a nearby wall and cuffing my hands behind my back. It all happened so fast. One moment I was standing on the sidewalk, thinking of the film, coffee, and catching Jake at the Gold Post before he'd met some young blond guy and conned him into going home with him to see his new pet iguana (that was his current pick-up routine, to take men home with him and introduce them to his iguana, a second Jake, named after himself as a reference to The Two Jakes, the long awaited sequel to the film Chinatown—Jake was a huge Nicholson fan). The next moment I was sitting in the back seat of a squad car, behind a metal mesh screen listening to the police radio, while one of West Hollywood's finest spoke my driver's license information into the microphone. I looked out the rear window toward the spot on the sidewalk where I'd just been standing to find Miyumi, my Japanese roommate staring back at me with a look of fear and curiosity, anxiety and suspicion. Knowing what I did about both Miyumi's traditional Japanese upbringing and her newly found Scientology teachings, I realized the questions that must have been going through her mind: Why had the police stopped me? What had I done to cause it? Did she really even know who I was? What seven steps does one follow to quickly resolve such a situation? And then, more importantly: Were the neighbors watching? Had she lost face?

"What are you holding me for?" I finally managed to ask. For the first time in my life, the hour-long lecture by Old Mr. Baxter, my high school civics teacher, on the writ of habeas corpus had some practical application for me. Unfortunately, the officers hadn't known Old Mr. Baxter nor his equivalent in their high schools. Or if they had, they'd already forgotten that particular lesson. Neither of them responded to my question. Instead, they simply continued listening to the radio, which I decided was probably in my best interest as well.

We didn't have to listen long. Within a few minutes, the same officer who had cautiously approached me on the sidewalk—tall, dark hair, light mustache—opened his door, then mine. He let me out of the car and took the handcuffs off. "Sorry," he said flatly, "for the inconvenience." Remembering he'd not yet answered the one question I'd dared to ask, I posed it a second time. "Why," I said, "did you pick me up?" The officer apologized again, this time adding in the same monotone voice, that they, he and his partner, had seen two black men dashing down an alleyway. They appeared to be running from some sort of crime. The officer "clarified" his rational to me not at all as I might have done to him had our roles been reversed—sheepishly, that is to say, a bit embarrassed at my ensuing behavior—but with the same empty expression he'd held throughout the entire ordeal, as if his actions and those of his partner were simply a matter of protocol. The suspects: suspicious looking black men running down a dark alleyway. Me: black man walking casually down a well-lit sidewalk in penny-loafers. I couldn't have run far—or fast for that matter—in those shoes if the sinister-looking black men the officers were looking for had actually been chasing me. My sudden anger compressed rapidly into a fist. Trapped inside my stomach, it ricocheted from wall to wall like a metal pinball flying against an endless number of rubber bumpers. There was no outlet. For I knew if I expressed the indignation I felt, though righteous, it might land me back in the squad car behind that metal grill. Or worse still, back in the alley those black men had run from, only I might not be seen later running out.

From the time we are children, we as black men are taught by our families and our communities to tread cautiously in both rural and urban jungles where racially motivated, predatory attitudes have not yet found their way onto the endangered species list. So for me, as well as many other black men and women, the fact that a group of white police officers would track down and brutally beat a black man for having sped on a city freeway, or an interstate highway, or mountain road, or even in his own front yard or driveway for that matter, carries with it no surprise. Even the rarest among us who have not yet had the unfortunate experience of being the focus of overly aggressive, suspicious, or hostile attitudes from white law-enforcement officers know people who have.

So no, I wasn't surprised by the Rodney King beating, only relieved that somehow, someone finally caught the abuse on tape. And that, I suppose, is where the complacency began. So—OK—yes. What follows now is a bit of a confession, an excuse really. For complacency in terms of human rights, liberty, and both collective and individual freedom is something that I have been warned against my entire life. My parents and siblings have made it their duty never to be just that. Worse still, I was naïve. Somehow I let myself believe that though I knew these sorts of law enforcement crimes still existed, once there was concrete, undeniable evidence of such injustices that our society—a society as modern and progressive as Los Angeles no less—would act swiftly to correct them. And this was to be the perfect example. In the case of Rodney King, I could keep all of my energy focused on trying to satisfy my lover, dealing with those nasty cable "Tiers," and making my new car payment, a BMW five-hundred series I'd bought to ease the stress of my daily Long Beach to Santa Monica commute. I could keep all of my energy focused on these things because in this case the incident was captured on video (yes, video. God bless America!). Because, I told myself, that if a picture is worth a thousand words, a video is worth what—just think about it—a thousand thousands! An open and shut case.

But now there were sirens, and Dionci was shaking her head and screaming in my office, her long beaded braids slapping hard against her back. And shit, I still had to get all the way back to Long Beach. I turned the TV off, grabbed my keys, shut the door, locked it, and walked Dionci out to her car.

"Don't worry about coming in tomorrow," I said (the inexperience of a young manager, I didn't know what else to say), "just take care of your home." Dionci stopped walking for a minute, looked back at me with the appropriate are-you-crazy-as-if-they-actually-pay-me-enough-here-to-worry-about-anything-right-now look, then continued toward her car.

The traffic didn't move. Every working man and woman living or working on the Westside, or in one of LA's many outlying beach communities had the same idea as Dionci and I. Under normal commuter circumstances, to get from Santa Monica to Long Beach took me anywhere from forty minutes to an hour. I simply caught the 10 freeway east at Bundy Drive and then the 405 freeway south to Orange Street, Cherry, or Spring. But that day, getting from my office to Bundy Drive and the 10 freeway—about four blocks—alone took close to an hour. Maybe more. And on the 10, getting from Bundy to the 405 interchange took equal the time. Once there, I had only two options: to take the 405 South, my normal route, now basically a parking lot for as far as I could see, or to continue east on the10, toward downtown and catch the 110 freeway to San Pedro, which meant cutting through South Central LA—the heart of all of the conflict. The first route didn't seem to be much of a choice at all, I was too anxious to get home. So, not fully realizing the implications of my impatience, I opted for the latter.

Without surprise, the 10 freeway leading into downtown was virtually empty. The lanes leading out, however, were packed. A mass exodus of people in cars sat trapped in unmoving traffic, their panic restrained solely by nylon straps wrapped over their shoulders and across their laps. Desperate to escape the rising pillars of smoke rapidly spreading behind them, none of the drivers looked back. Gripping their steering wheels tight, they stared anxiously forward toward their suburban refuges, afraid that a single glance behind might turn them too, like the city they were fleeing, into a pillar of smoke. All the while I drove toward it. Having already past the 405 it was too late for me to change my course.

Swarms of helicopters with pointed tails painted in shades of orange and black, some with white stripes circled above and beyond me. In their frenzy, they dodged in and out of the spreading flames like a host of hornets trying to recover their burning hives. Before my eyes, the sky turned quickly from blue to rusty red, from orange to charcoal gray. By the time I reached the downtown 110 exchange, it seemed I'd witnessed the full transition of day to sunset, then night. Surrounded on both sides of the freeway by rising flames and smoke, the sound of police cars, ambulances, and helicopters, I was lost; the city I thought I knew no longer existed. I tried desperately to place myself within the landscape that now surrounded me but my inability to do so, to integrate what I was seeing with what I knew to be real, forced me back into that ephemeral state of disbelief I'd previously been driven out of in my office by Dionci.

What surrounded me now was not LA, but an unreal city. The fact that I was much closer to the violence of the riots now than I had been in my office did not dissuade my disbelief. On the contrary, the proximity reinforced it.

In order to keep going, to not break down in fear, or sadness, or utter derangement, my denial had to be stronger. As my physical temperature began to climb, I simply turned the air-conditioner up. I was no longer watching the events from behind my desk, but had driven directly into the box. And the box, a still inner voice reminded me, was just a stage. This was all a wartime Hollywood film set complete with special effects, sound bytes, and props. I was now—again—a spectator and regarded the scenes around me with newly found since of dramatic awe, a distance untouched by the panic so evident in the faces of those I'd left behind me heading west on the Santa Monica freeway. I was calm.

The 110 offramps bordering South Central LA had all been blocked off by the time I reached them. Not that I needed any of them anyway, I was headed much farther down. And once out of this quarantined area there was a sort of normality. I had, without immediately realizing it, passed the point where the smoke was getting denser and denser, and arrived to where it trailed a good distance behind me. Soon the real sunset approached and, at the base of the 110 freeway, I crossed the bridge between San Pedro and Long Beach looking out toward the pier. I drove Ocean Boulevard toward home with the open beach on one side of me and neatly arranged California bungalow-styled homes on the other. The sky was clear; and I parked my car one block up from Ocean, in front of my duplex on 1st Street. I stuck the key in the door lock and, without even twisting the handle, it swung opened before me. Scott, my lover, was standing on the other side. He grabbed me and threw his arms around my neck.

"My god!" he said, he squeezed me tight. "Why didn't you call me before you left the office?"

Behind him, against the back wall of the room, the TV was on. He had been watching the live coverage of the riots. I felt panic in his grip, and realized how real everything I'd just passed through had been, the very possibility of danger in the streets I'd driven through. The helicopters, the fire, the smoke I thought I'd left behind had been at home waiting for me in that box. That big black box that was always on everywhere. That damn box that made fiction of things that were important and real, and real those things that weren't. I pushed Scott away from me and ran across the room to turn the TV off.

"Are you OK?" he said. And I began to cry. I looked around the room, at the TV, at all the new furniture and lighting we'd only just bought, and then back up at Scott.

"Are you OK?" he said. And I realized, the sirens still ringing in my ears, that I'd paid too much for everything.

REFLECTIONS ON OUTRAGE IN THE STREET

Elizabeth Wong

The man took a quick deep breath, aimed, and spat on us. The spittle ricocheted off the right shoulder of my leather jacket and landed, full-bodied and glistening, in Stacy's long, wavy hair.

With no tissue between us, we were forced to wear it, like a brooch and a barrette. And by the time we arrived at our destination, it had dried.

A full year later, I now realize how different my reaction was to this event, compared with the reaction of my friend Stacy, perhaps telling about the complicated nature of race relations. The man was African-American, Stacy is Polish-American, and I am Chinese-American.

The incident happened last May. The atmosphere in New York City was electric, rife with rumor and fear. You could feel it everywhere. It was a few days after the acquittal in the Rodney King beating trial. Los Angeles was burning, and New York was nervous.

I was working part-time, selling kimonos in a boutique. On my way to lunch, sales people and store owners were standing outside, looking worried, facing midtown, the Chrysler Building in the distance.

"They are shooting at police helicopters," one person told me.

"I heard they were rioting inside Madison Square Garden," another said.

"We're closing early," several people told me. "Not so much that they'll come here, but some of us have to get home."

They who? Who were they? I went back to the store and listened to the radio. Announcers on several stations reported in. No one was shooting at police helicopters. The subway stations, the major thoroughfares of the city had not shut down. There was, indeed, a skirmish at Madison Square Garden, but it was a minor case of vandalism, no one injured.

Rumor had spread like wildfire, by word of mouth, by fax, by telephone. Stacy called and told me that everyone at her law office was going home early. I told her I was still going to Jennifer's art opening. No slave to fear and rumor, are we? She agreed to come along.

Stacy is your basic good egg: a Master's degree in liberal arts, kind to animals, loves babies. She looks into the eyes of street people, tries to see all points of view, likes ethnic foods and ethnic men. Raphael or Botticelli might have painted her flowing blonde hair, her aristocratic nose, her dreamy far-off expression.

As we walked down Broadway, the black man approached. He appeared raggedy, with a stubby graying beard and shabby oversized sports coat. He was muttering to himself. And as he approached, Stacy—uncharacteristically—whispered, "Maybe we should cross the street?" But before I could consider the suggestion, the man scooted toward us and spat. "Whitey. Chink," he said. And moved on.

Stacy burst into tears. I looked for a tissue.

"How could he do that?" she said. "How dare he do that? He just judged us like that, based on our color. He doesn't know me. I give money to guys like that. I smile and say hello to guys like that."

I listened. I didn't cry. I wasn't outraged. Where was my outrage?

I was thinking about getting to the reception, and about the last time someone spat on me. On a San Francisco street, ages ago, an old Chinese man, also with a stubby graying beard and shabby clothing, spat and called me a whore as I walked hand-in-hand with blond, blue-eyed Oliver.

I cried then. I was outraged then.

But now, it doesn't shock me. I have been refused service in restaurants. I have lost promotions. I have been underestimated as an artist and overlooked as a potential marital mate, solely because of my color.

The converse also has been true. I have had preferential treatment in restaurants, gotten jobs, been touted as an artist, and sought by men as desirable, solely based on the color of my skin.

True, the content of my character or the integrity of my actions are, thankfully, sometimes factored in. But on the whole, no one has given me anything or taken something away without considering my race. Nothing has come to me solely on merit. I have learned to accept this as a fact of my life. I couldn't be angry at the man who spat at me. I knew he had been asking "How dare they?" all his life. I had been socialized to accept inequities, but someday, might I reach a boiling point too? Might I lash out? Spit?

Stacy was still in shock. "How can you be so calm?" she asked. "What's the matter with your? It's not like stuff like this happens every day."

"Oh really?" I replied.

Stacy was silent. After awhile, she stopped, held me by the arm, and said, "Stuff like this happens all the time to people of color, doesn't it? I'm privileged, in a way, aren't I? Stuff like this happens all the time, especially if you're black. Am I right? That's why people are in the streets in LA, right?"

Stacy composed herself. We looked at some good paintings and talked about art as we walked home. The streets were quiet, littered with glass from storefront windows broken during a solidarity march that day.

Stacy and I never spoke of the incident again.

BIOS

Pat Alderete's short stories are published in *Joteria* and *Pen Center Journal*, and anthologized in *Hers 2 and 3* and in *Los Angeles Gay and Lesbian Latino Arts Anthology 1988~2000*. Her one-act play, *Ghost and the Spirit*, was produced as a staged reading in 1997, and her one-woman performance, *Tina Gets Married*, was produced in 1999.

Lisa Alvarez is a professor of English at Irvine Valley College and is co-director of the fiction program at the Squaw Valley Community of Writers.

Florentino Apeles has been in the gas station business for more than thirty years. Because of his first job as a sales rep for Esso (Exxon) in the Philippines, he developed a serious obsession with tigers—but his true passion is singing. His two Los Angeles gas stations also sell sing-a-long equipment and his custom-designed karaoke systems.

Teena Apeles is a writer, editor, and book artist. Her nonfiction book *Cool Women: Warriors* will be published by Girl Press in 2002. She co-founded Spin the Wheel Press, a collaborative venture by Los Angeles-based artists and writers to develop innovative projects and experimental texts including *The Deck of Chance* and the *Collage* series. Her next publishing venture is *Timid*, a magazine targeting the shy intellectual.

Pamela Jo Balluck left Los Angeles in 1993. She received her BA in creative writing from the University of Montana at Missoula; an MFA in writing fiction at the University of Utah, and is currently completing a novel-in-stories while working on her Ph.D. at Utah. Her stories have appeared in the *Western Humanities Review* and *Quarter After Eight*. This is her first non-fiction publication.

Lili Barsha is a writer of fiction, poetry, and plays, who also acts and produces live theater. Her works include *365 Days of Humiliation, a year in the life of an actress* (excerpts published by *Asahi Shimbun* in 1997); *Sextrology*, a monthly astrology column for BOLD Magazine; *Lili Barsha's Haunted Cabaret*, a Halloween variety show; and *Cabaret Love*, a Valentine-themed poetry and musical revue produced each year in Los Angeles.

Anne Beatts won two Emmys and three WGA Awards as a writer, creator, and producer for various television shows, including *Saturday Night Live*. Her work on Broadway includes *Gilda Live* and the Tony-nominated musical *Leader of the Pack*. She co-wrote several books, including *TITTERS 101*. Her work has appeared in *Vogue, Elle, Esquire, Playboy*, and the *Los Angeles Times*. She lives in Los Angeles.

Phillip Brock is a writer and an actor living in Echo Park with Ellen and Edison in an old house on a hill.

Associate editor for *Turning Point Magazine*, **Shonda Buchanan** is a fiction writer, essayist, performance artist, and poet, currently working on a memoir, *Willow Women*. The recipient of the Sundance Institute Writing Program Fellowship, she freelances for *L.A. Weekly* and the *Los Angeles Times* and commentates for *Marketplace Radio*. Her work has been published in several books including *Bum Rush the Page: A Def Poetry Jam*.

Wanda Coleman was born in Watts and raised in South Central LA. Her work appears in several collections, including *A War of Eyes* (stories), *Native in a Strange Land* (prose), *Mambo Hips and Make Believe* (a novel), and *Mercurochrome: New Poems* (2001 National Book Award bronze-medalist). Her honors include the 1990 Harriette Simpson Arnow Prize (*The American Voice*) and the 1999 Lenore Marshall Prize presented by The Academy of American Poets and *The Nation* for *Bathwater Wine* (poems).

Cara Mia DiMassa is a staff writer at the *Los Angeles Times*. She is a graduate of Georgetown University's School of Foreign Service.

Kitty Felde hosts NPR affiliate KPCC's afternoon talk show, *Talk of the City*. She is an award-winning public radio journalist with seventeen years experience. She also covered the International Criminal Tribunals for the former Yugoslavia and Rwanda, logging more time in the courtroom than any other American reporter. Also a playwright, her work about Teddy Roosevelt's daughter *ALICE* premiered at Washington's National Theater. Ms. Felde teaches playwriting to inner-city kids in Los Angeles.

Ramón García is a professor at California State University at Northridge. His poetry and short fiction has appeared in a variety of journals and anthologies including *Best American Poetry* 1996, *The Paterson Literary Review*, *The Floating Borderland: 25 Years of Hispanic Literature in the United States*, *Urban Latino Cultures*, *The Americas Review*, *Virgins, Guerrillas and Locas: Gay Latinos Writing About Love*, and *Story*.

Lynell George is a journalist living in Los Angeles. A feature writer for the *Los Angeles Times*, her work has also appeared in various newspapers and magazines including the *Washington Post*, the *Boston Globe*, *L.A. Weekly*, *Essence*, and *Vibe*.

Victoria Gutierrez-Kovner, LCSW, is a bilingual/bicultural Licensed Clinical Social Worker in the Pasadena area. She has extensive experience working with children, adolescents, adults, couples, and families. Her specialties include child abuse, sexual abuse, violence, trauma, and cultural diversity. She also provides consultation and training related to the above issues.

Gar Anthony Haywood is the Shamus and Anthony Award-winning author of eight mystery novels. Six feature African-American private investigator Aaron Gunner, and two recount the adventures of Joe and Dottie Loudermilk, Airstream-owning crime solvers in constant flight from their five troublesome children. Haywood, who has written for television, and both the *Los Angeles Times* and *New York Times*, lives with his wife and two daughters in the Silver Lake area of his native Los Angeles.

Erin Aubry Kaplan is a staff writer and columnist for the *L.A. Weekly* whose work has appeared in the *Los Angeles Times*, the *New Times*

Los Angeles, VIBE, and others. The former host of KPFK's morning news show, "Up For Air" and PEN WEST's award winner for journalism in 2000, her poetry has been published in *Spectrum*, and her essays have been published in multiple books, most recently *Step into a World: A Global Anthology of Black Literature*.

James J. Koch lives, and writes, in Southern California.

Larry Kronish was born and raised in LA. He attended UCSB College of Creative Studies, spent three and a half years living and working in Japan, and currently teaches public high school in LA. He has two yet unpublished novels, *The Sushi King's Daughter* and *Firelight*, and is currently working on *Mortal's Delight*, a book of tales.

Eric Lax is the author of *Life and Death on 10 West, Woody Allen: A Biography*, and, with A.M. Sperber, *Bogart*. He is a member of the boards of Pen USA West and International Pen.

Adolfo Guzman Lopez was born in Mexico City but left the best years of his childhood in the *colonias* of Tijuana and National City, California. With The Taco Shop Poets he took poetry to *taquerias* and cultural centers from California to New York's Spanish Harlem. By day, Adolfo impersonates a public radio reporter and by night he wanders the streets of Los Angeles trying to find the right words for the sounds he hears.

Peter Maunu trained in violin and guitar at the San Francisco Conservatory of Music. He became an in demand guitarist, recording and performing with artists including Jean-Luc Ponty, Tony Williams, Bobby McFerrin, and Joni Mitchell. He was co-founder of the innovative Group 87 with Mark Isham, Patrick O'Hearn, and Terry Bozzio. A member of Arsenio Hall's "Posse", he accompanied musicians from Ray Charles to Ringo Starr. He has recorded two solo albums and continues session work on recording film and television scores.

A naturalized Calibronian, **Donna Mungen's** work has appeared in *USA Today, L.A. Weekly*, the *Los Angeles Times*, and others. Her commentaries have aired on *All Things Considered* and *CNN-TV*. She received first place as Investigative Reporter from the Greater Los Angeles Press Club and covered the O.J. Simpson trial for the *New York Times*. Her A&E documentary, *Masada*, received a Cable Ace nomination. She is currently a professor of English at Pasadena City College.

Luis Paquime was born in 1968. He grew up in Los Angeles and served five years in the Army, two active and three with the National Guard. He has taught elementary school in Los Angeles County for five years, and has written an unpublished novel about the 1992 Los Angeles Riots.

Kristin L. Petersen is a third-generation LA native and editor of the 2nd Edition of *Hungry? Los Angles: The Lowdown on Where the Real People Eat!*. She is also a writer, artist, and managing editor of the Glove Box Guides.

Robert Petersen was fifteen years old and lived in Pasadena during the 1992 Los Angeles Uprising. He is currently a musician playing bass with the Robert Petersen Quintet, Gwendolyn, and Quazar and the Bamboozled. He is also the Director of Programs for the Fair Housing Council of San Gabriel Valley, a legal advocacy organization that fights against housing discrimination. He currently lives in Angeleno Heights.

Gary D. Phillips writes stories about crime, mysteries, and politics. Visit his web site at www.gdphillips.com.

Cynthia Adam Prochaska teaches composition and literature at Mount San Antonio College. Her short stories have appeared in the *Florida Review* and the *Santa Monica Review*.

A Southern California native, **Renée A. Ruiz** considers her life something between a Sandra Cisneros story and purgatory. She longs to capture the conflict resulting from a sense of transience and a need to belong. She sees herself as an Aztec warrior princess trapped in a valley girl, the consequence of being too brown, but not brown enough. A graduate of UC Davis' Creative Writing Program, she resides in Northern California with her daughter and fiancé.

Greg Sarris received his Ph.D. in Modern Thought and Literature from Stanford University. He has published several books of essays and fiction, including his most recent, critically acclaimed novel, *Watermelon Nights*. He has written and adapted works for television and film, and is Chairman of his American Indian tribe, the Federated Indians of the Graton Rancheria. Formerly a professor of English at UCLA, he is now Professor of Creative Writing and Literature at Loyola Marymount University.

Christian T. Sierra is a novelist, journalist, teacher, and native Angeleno. He currently lives with his wife, Kerri Hinkle, in Tucson, Arizona. His work has appeared in several magazines and journals throughout the United States, most recently in *The Tucson Weekly*. He is currently working on a historical novel set in Sonora, Mexico.

T.E. Spence lives with his wife and a feral cat in Glendale, California.

Andrew Tonkovich is a writer, teacher, and activist. He edits the nationally distributed literary arts journal the *Santa Monica Review*.

David L. Ulin is the editor of *Another City: Writing from Los Angeles* and the author of *Cape Cod Blues*, a book of poems. His work has appeared in *L.A. Weekly*, the *Los Angeles Times*, *The Nation*, *GQ*, *The Atlantic Monthly*, *The New York Times Book Review*, and on National Public Radio's *All Things Considered*.

Marco Villalobos is a fool who fans culture's flames. The poet and writer lived in Southern California during the '92 insurrection, but has since gone dolo for broke in Brooklyn. In between columns of smoke rising from the bellies of LA and New York, he has written for *Stress*, *Code*, and now, the *Fader Magazine*. A collection of his work entitled *Lolo Bikes that Bounce* is forthcoming.

Oscar Villalon is the book editor for the *San Francisco Chronicle*. He lives in San Francisco.

Scott Wannberg is a member of Robert Viharo's ongoing process of a workshop. He graduated from San Francisco State University and believes in Strother Martin.

Ellery Washington C. studied liberal arts at Pepperdine University and architecture at the University of New Mexico. He has worked in architecture and advertising, and in 1995, co-founded Sine Modo Films, an independent documentary film company. His short fiction haws appeared in *Puerto del Sol*, *The Quarterly*, *The Berkeley Fiction Review*, *Fiction9*, and *Griots Beneath the Baobub*, an anthology of African-American writers. He currently divides his time between Los Angeles and Paris, France.

Elizabeth Wong, playwright, has an MFA from New York University's Tisch School of the Arts. Her plays include *Letters to a Student, Revolutionary, Kimchee & Chitlins, The Happy Prince, Boid & Oskar*, all published by Dramatic Publishing Co. She's listed in the *Dictionary of Literary Biography* and the *Oxford Who's Who of Women Writers*. She's a member of Pen West, the Dramatist Guild, and Writers Guild West.